Ba.naf.sheh
noun

THE COLOUR
VIOLET

An Iranian Woman's Journey Across Two
Continents In A Quest For Her Freedom

"If you are what you should be, you will set this whole world on fire."

- St. Catherine of Siena

Chapters

The Human Spirit 2

Bandar Abbas 23

Farhad 33

From Rasht to Hamilton 45

F*CK Cancer 58

Blended Family 83

Return to Tehran 95

"I do" 109

My New Chapter 119

Divorce Papers 132

Meeting the Devil 148

Iran 173

The Human Spirit

The Persian poet Rumi wrote, "You are not a drop in the ocean. You are the entire ocean in a drop". Historians agree that the world's first superpower was the Persian Empire founded by Cyrus the Great around 550 B.C. It united the governance of three ancient civilizations – Mesopotamia, Egypt's Nile Valley, and India's Indus Valley. These fertile lands hold the rich heritage of my ancestry. Centuries of people guided by the beautiful verses of Rumi etched across mountainous landscapes and the Persian Gulf. My family immigrated from Iran to Canada when I was twelve years old. I have since travelled back to Iran twice; the first to get married and the second to bury him.

The human spirit is a powerful force. I am convinced that one day we will be able to measure its energy in Joules or its force in Newtons. When I think about the origins of my human spirit, my innate energy and force, they were woven into my fabric from my early childhood in Iran by my father, baba, and mother, maman. Baba is the kindest person that I have ever known. His human spirit directed his focus on helping the people around him. Growing up, Baba's father worked for Iran Railways as a station manager, and as such things go, it involved moving from one city to another along with his father's postings. This afforded him the luxury of understanding the diverse landscape and people of Iran and to respect differences among people, something he emulates even today. Baba was a smart student who was admitted to the University of Shihraz, enrolling in their prestigious agriculture program, and as the program was to be in English, he had to register himself in several intensive English language courses. It was in taking these courses that he fell in love with the language, so much so that he eventually transferred out of the agriculture program and graduated with a BA in English. There's a song in the musical Avenue Q that asks, "What do you do with a BA in English?" Well, they should have interviewed baba for the answer. Baba built an entire life around this language, and it would eventually seep into my veins as well. He owned and operated a private English language school, taught at a local university, and performed numerous translations of official government documents. One of my fondest childhood memories with baba involved him notarizing his translated documents at the local courts. We would walk there together, and after he had finished, he would take me to the bazaar where we would enjoy a Pirashki and a banana milkshake. A Pirashki is a delicious Iranian pastry of deep-fried dough filled with a cream custard. The pairing with an ice-cold banana milkshake would freeze my little five-year old brain as baba and I would talk and laugh our way home. It was on one of these walks, I asked him why leaves fell to the ground. "Every object which has mass is physically attracted to every other object that has mass", he said. Baba continued as I tried to keep up, "You see this parked car, it has a force of attraction to that car which is parked across the street, just like every object in the universe has this physical attraction to every other object. And the bigger the mass the greater the force". Baba went on to what I presume was explaining that since Earth's mass was so much larger than every object on Earth, like the leaf, all objects fell towards the Earth by this force of attraction. But I lost his train of thought somewhere around everything being attracted to everything else and spent the remainder of the conversation taking comfort in knowing that Baba and I would always be pulled together wherever we were. From a young age, he made a point to always speak to me like an adult, and it was then that he introduced me to Isaac Newton's discovery of gravity. In the Farsi language, there are two subject pronouns – singular and plural. The plural pronoun is used formally and to indicate respect. This is particularly true within Iranian culture, where it is almost demanded when addressing elders, while the singular pronoun is used to address kids and people of lower social standing. Baba always addressed me with the plural pronoun, while I would use the singular pronoun for him. This is our relationship - to this day he calls me Banoojaan. This is my baba – respectful towards all, patient, and always polite.

Maman's human spirit was like none other, as she was a match for no one, maybe not even baba, but somehow, he became the luckiest man in the world. Although Maman's family came from wealth and status, by the time I was born, all that money was lost to failed businesses and family disputes. I would frequently hear about a distant relative going to the royal court to settle a dispute or resolve some matter. It could have been a generation old inheritance conflict, or property settlement, but even as a child, I understood that it was the family's social standing which allowed entry to the royal courts even if only for minor dealings.

Maman was the daughter of a man who had, at most, four years of formal education, and a woman who had none. Maman, however, was brilliant. She was intent on becoming an engineer, and like baba, attended the prestigious University of Shihraz for Mechanical Engineering.

Unsurprisingly, she was the only woman in her class, she graduated at the top of her class with a master's degree in Mechanical Engineering. I had always attributed maman's academic success to being a hardworking and meticulous student. This was until recently, when my aunt told me that although she barely studied, she was certainly the brightest and most gifted in the class. Maman graduated from university before the Islamic Revolution of 1979 and her first job was with the government of Iran in their Nuclear program. I never really understood then what she did, but thirty years later, knowing more about Iran's nuclear program, I wish I had paid more attention. Growing in her career, maman would be promoted and eventually become the Chief Safety Officer for the Ministry of Labour in our province. Her team's role was to protect and advocate for the rights of the workers in the province.

In elementary school, I would always return home before both of my parents came back from work. Our nanny would hand me the radio as she prepared lunch. I would hastily turn it on and tune in to my favourite channel, where I would listen to the voice of maman talking with community leaders about the importance of protecting our workers, and demanding local and international businesses adhere to the highest standards of safety at work for their employees. I understood one out of every ten sentences spoken by maman and the interviewer, but it didn't take much to realize that my maman was different.

People gravitated towards her because of her genuine energy and care for everyone, and how she made everyone felt, seen, and heard. Learning early on about gravity, I assumed this was the gravitational pull baba taught me, seeing groups of adults flock around maman to hear her speak. When my parents were trying to move to another city, the community and her workplace made many flattering requests attempting to dissuade them. Maman was captivating in her presence and charismatic with her words. To this day, I have never met anyone like her. She was the center of every room whether she was speaking or not. She truly was a living legend, and I knew very early on that maman was someone to be shared for the greater need of the community. I didn't like this understanding, because like every young child, I wanted maman all to myself. You couldn't escape any gathering without someone sharing a story or praise about maman. There was no shortage of stories about Behjat Taghikhani. While Maman started her career wearing miniskirts, by the time her career ended in Iran and we were immigrating to Canada, there were so many religious reforms invoked in Iran that she would have to be covered from head to toe in black. The woman under the veil however, never changed.

Maman had an interesting way of talking and gathering information. When I was around five years old, while sitting on a chair with my hands tucked under my seat, I ended up cutting my hand on one of the projecting screws. When maman heard my scream and came into the room, her first question was – "Banoo, how did the chair do that to you?" She always gave people the benefit of the doubt, to explain their version of the story and the most important thing for her in every encounter was for everyone's story to be heard.

One evening my family was out for a picnic and when we returned to our neighbourhood, we learned that there had been a burglary in the community and several homes, including ours, were broken into As other people panicked, maman was outside talking to everyone and calming our neighbours, a lot of whom didn't even have their homes broken into but were shocked by the events. That was her human spirit, always guided by putting the needs of others first and caring for the larger community.

My favourite memories with maman were during my birthdays. She would take the day off, pull me out of school for the day, and we would spend the entire day together, shopping, cooking, and getting ready for my birthday party in the evening. We would clean the home and get the decorations up and buy every kind of food and drink that I wanted, and she would dedicate her day to me. Maman was unlike other women in my neighbourhood because she spent a lot of time on her career. But when she was with me and at home, she made every moment count. For maman, I was Banoo, and for me she was Superwoman!

Baba and maman couldn't be any more different. Maman was energetic, and baba was calm. Maman was a driven engineering student and baba was a partying rebel who was kicked out of classes. They should never have met. But against all odds, they met in a judo class in university. Baba was the coach and maman the student. Baba had one job as a coach, and it was to not flirt with the girls in the class and he failed at that. Of course, baba doesn't describe it as flirting. "With your maman, it was different", he would always say. "It was love, and I knew that I was going to marry her". Baba was 6 months and 6 days older than maman and growing up I always thought that was the greatest cosmic coincidence. They got married in Tehran, after baba's mandatory military assignment, in maman's parents' home. Maman did her own hair and make-up for the small and private celebration.

Growing up my parents' marriage was the perfect relationship in my eyes. I never saw them fight or raise their voices at each other, at us, or anyone else. Baba would always quote Rumi and say, "Raise your words, not your voice. It is rain that grows flowers, not thunder". The only time that I would hear maman upset was when she saw baba working while he was sick. Only then would she raise her voice in a plea to ask him to take care of himself and rest. When I was seven years old, I was watching a Bollywood movie dubbed in Farsi with maman and the woman on the screen was crying and being melodramatic about making a point that her children were the most important people in her life. I don't remember anything else about the movie, but after it was done

I quickly jumped to confirm with maman that I was the most important person in her life and I was so excited to hear her validation. But instead she said, "Banoo, I love you, but your baba is the most important and my favourite person. See when baba and I decided to have children, we didn't know who was going to arrive and how our children would be. I had no choice over that matter. But I willingly and intentionally chose baba exactly how he was, to be my partner." It was them against the world. They left Tehran in pursuit of their careers and took turns supporting each other's ambitions. If there was anything that one of them wanted, the other would do everything in their power to bring it to life. They always had each other's back and as a child it was nearly impossible to play them against each other.

Their affection was not just behind closed doors and only for their children to witness. During dinner parties, where the men and women would sit separately and have their own conversations, my parents would be in the center of the room, sitting together and always holding hands. They were crazy about each other and couldn't envision life without each other. Unfortunately, a lot sooner than they both had planned, they would have to prepare for that outcome.

Most people say that you can tell that I am a middle child and that I suffer from 'middle child syndrome'. The unofficial definition of middle-child syndrome is feeling isolated because the perception is parents love the oldest the most as they came first of course, and they spoil the youngest, leaving you in the alone. I never felt this way. I was the center of my parents' universe and there was no doubt about it. My older sister was eight years older than me and her mannerisms were too foreign for me to understand or relate to. While I have faint memories from our childhood of watching Bollywood movies together, most of my clearest memories are of fighting with her and repeatedly wishing that we were not siblings. Being so much older than me, she would be allowed to go away for sleepovers with my other cousins in different towns and the only thought in my head when this would happen is wishing that she never returned. Once when I was ten years old, we got into a huge fight because she emptied an entire bottle of ketchup onto my hair and to make things worse, decorated it with salt. Quite literally adding salt to the wound. It was two in the morning and although that incident sealed the deal for me, I knew well before that incident that Bahar and me would not have a fond childhood together. Later when I was eight years old, and she sixteen, I remember there was a loud thunderstorm, and I was scared and just wanted some elderly protection at night. So, I asked if I could sleep with her on her bed and all she would afford to me was allowing me to sleep on the ground beside her bed, like a dog. She used to call me Banooleh when we were younger, a name invented by our cousin Farhad.

When I was five years old my parents gave me the best news that I had gotten up until that moment. We were getting a little brother. I remember being so excited from the second I knew about his existence. I would fold and refold his onesies in preparation for his arrival. The night of Kasra's birth is as clear as yesterday. The neighbours were over at our house to watch Bahar and me while my parents were at the hospital. I loved him like my own baby, although I was only six years old when he was born. We would play together all the time and as he got older, I would begin to introduce him to all my hobbies and interests. I learned and developed the understanding of the emotion to protect someone from being Kasra's older sister. Throughout my childhood, I would have dreams about protecting or saving a young boy in some grave and unrealistic alternate universe scenario. Although in my dreams the face of the young boy might be distorted or unrecognizable, I always woke up knowing it was Kasra. Subconsciously, Kasra must have felt this comfort and protection from me as well, because to this day, he is the only person who calls me by my full first name, Banafsheh.

My name is Banafsheh Karbalaei. My human spirit has always been a genetic combination of maman and baba. I am a confident conversationalist like maman, and a rule breaker like baba. I am rarely ever the follower in a group, but always the leader of the pack. Growing up, my two closest friends were Satareh and Mojdeh and they followed me everywhere. My childhood was predictable. We spent a lot of time near the Persian Gulf, in fish markets, and indulging in gheyr-e behdashti, Iranian street food. I never did my homework, but I loved reading. Our home had a huge library, and I would spend countless hours inside these books. I was obsessed with Persian history, the lives of its kings and queens, and the majestic Persian empire. In fact, it would be accurate to call me a dramatic child, who was largely influenced by the books I read and the melodramatic Bollywood movies I watched.

Bandar Abbas

Iran.-

Or The Islamic Republic of Iran.

I know what people think about my country. Dictatorship. Religious extremists. Nuclear weapons. Oppressive culture. Covered women.

However, growing up in Iran was somehow far away from any of these controversies. My childhood was filled with hot days, and warm nights. Surrounded by colourful clothes, palm trees, and the beautiful Persian Gulf. My family moved from Tehran to a coastal city called Bandar Abbas where I was born and spent the most glorious first eight years of my life. Bandar Abbas is on the Persian Gulf, about an hour's flight from Dubai. This city made headline news in 1988, when Iran Air's Flight 655 was shot down over it's airspace by USS Vincennes, a guided-missile cruiser of the United States Navy. Despite this happening when I was only a year old, I would repeatedly hear this story recited by adults at parties, and teachers in classrooms, for many years to come. If you were old enough to remember what did occur, you always remembered exactly what you were doing when it happened. There are a few such world events that immediately come into my memory: 9/11 while in my first week of high school, and the death of my favourite artist Prince while at a café in downtown Toronto. For my parents and their peers, this 1988 incident would be one of those defining world events. I was born towards the very end of the eight-year Iran-Iraq war after which my parents had moved to Bandar Abbas. It was a challenging time to live in Iran and raise a family. It was a war that defined our culture, rewrote our history, and created the present state of Iran. In the face of this adversity and a new child on its way, my parents moved to Bandar Abbas for a fresh new start.

Bandar Abbas was a lively city of Bandari people, an ethnic group that speak a dialect of Farsi. They are known for their colourful fabrics, which they used for their clothes, linens, and drapes. The colours were light like the wind that travels from the gulf over the land. They were often transparent and had the most beautiful patterns. Bandari people always covered themselves fully, not due to religious demand, but because of the oppressive heat. If there was only one adjective to describe Bandar Abbas, it would be that it was always very hot! It wasn't uncommon for temperatures to soar to fifty degrees Celsius in the summertime. Even for the women that wore a niqab, it was primarily out of choice to protect themselves from the heat. The accumulation of sweat inside your garments because of restricted air flow was preferred over exposed skin that would burn under the scorching sun. But even then, to remain fashionable was vital, and these niqabs were made of colourful, transparent, and vibrant printed fabrics. The Bandari people were a lively bunch. And this was primarily attributed to its coastal geography making it a renown international port, a primary source of business and the backbone of the city's economy. This port would bring international visitors at all times of the day and night. And with these ships arrived merchants, businesses, diverse cultures, international cuisines, and pop-music. All these imports made the Bandari people particularly educated, inclusive, open minded, and worldly. As a result, Bandar Abbas was very different to the rest of the country, especially Tehran. This international port also brought international TV channels. I distinctly remember maman's obsession with The Bold and The Beautiful, unwavering in her commitment to miss even a single episode of Eric Forrester and Brooke Logan. With all the international exposure and awareness also came its own set of dangers. Growing up it was very common to hear about child abductions in the news. This fear was instilled in our minds at a very young age and we knew that it was extremely dangerous to be outside of your home or school without supervision. It was also a common sight to see extreme poverty and even families of beggars on the streets. Very often the beggars were young children, about the same age as me, with one, or more limbs missing. My parents explained that these children were kidnapped from their homes and were being abused by manipulative adults to beg on the streets. There were entire economies and businesses created from this abuse.

Aside from this horror on the streets, life in Bandar Abbas was full of festivities. Bandaris had big, colourful weddings filled with music and dancing that lasted full weeks to enjoy both cultural and religious festivities. Outside of wedding festivities, all other social gatherings were primarily inside people's homes. Due to the heat, Bandari people would do anything to stay either indoors or near the water with the breeze. House parties with groups of friends were a common weekend activity and my parents were certainly the most well-known hosts in our neighbourhood. These parties would be themed like a masquerade or costume party where the guests would dress up elaborately and invest a lot of time to impress their hosts and the other guests. Every element of Bandari living was larger than life. And for when people gathered outside, it was inevitably near the water, to soak in the breeze from the sea. Groups of families would meet in green shaded areas under large trees very close to the beach. The kids would gather and play near the water while the adults would setup a hookah next to the park bench and barbequed kebabs. My family spent a lot of time near the water. A Saturday morning tradition would have us venturing out on to the beach with butter knives that we would bring from home. We would pierce the knives into the sand intermittently, and if it hit something hard, you would dig to retrieve your prize. Often this would find a clam shell. We would then collect these clams, take them back home, clean and cook them for Saturday lunch or dinner. The water in the gulf was clean and so my family spent many evenings and weekends together on the beach or out on speedboats without any life jackets. As I stated previously, the most glorious eight years of my life.

Life in Bandar Abbas, outside of attending school of course, were filled with these masquerade-style house parties, find-a-clam beach outings, and daily trips to the bazaar.

Need a sofa, welcome to the bazaar.

Running out of spices, see you at the bazaar.

Want to sew a new dress, head down to the bazaar.

I loved going with baba to the bazaar, especially as it meant riding in his big blue Chevy pick-up. The only one of its kind in our neighbourhood. It was bright and bold and well known by everyone. People would see me at school and mention how they saw baba driving down the main road the other day in his blue truck. And baba had installed two metal bars at the back of the truck that went across the two sides of the truck bed. These bars were meant to safely keep the items in the bed from rolling out while driving. And the items in the bed of the truck were mostly me and my siblings. We would jump at any opportunity to ride in the back with baba. It was always an adventure of getting rolled around as we drove through the pot-holed filled streets of Bandar Abbas. And of course, there were no seatbelts. This was Iran in the 1990s. People were free and felt invincible and that is the fire which still runs in my veins today.

Farhad

Iranian families, like most eastern cultures, are a large group of first cousins and second cousins and aunts and uncles and grandparents and so many others. My family was no different- the drama and sensitivities of hurt egos, the breaking up and making up of families was a regular in my big fat Iranian family. Growing up, we were closer to maman's side of the family who lived in Tehran. My grandparents were given made up names, that didn't mean grandma or grandpa. My "grandmother" was called

Takhanjoon and my "grandfather" was called "Afaghjoon". Takhanjoon and Afaghjoon had four children – Farjad, maman, Farshad, and Nazhat. My oldest Amoo, or uncle, Farjad, was a pilot who lived all over the world. I remember hearing stories about him and his family in Tokyo, Honolulu, Toronto, and many other famous cities around the world. It's tracing his travels from one part of the world map to another that taught me my world geography, the seven continents, and the four oceans. In fact, it was receiving his annual Eid cards, with their family pictures from all these different cities, that first introduced me to the idea of traveling. Amoo Farjad had two kids, but I would never really get too close to my cousins until many years later when our families would move to Canada at the same time.

My younger Amoo Farshad, was a lawyer who was single until around forty-five. And as it was the Iranian custom for unmarried children, he lived with my grandparents until then. Amoo Farshad did eventually marry and had one daughter. Due to the large difference in our age, I was never very close to her. Finally, there was maman's best friend and confidante, my favourite aunt Nazhat, whom we call Nazee with love. Nazee had divorced her husband before I was born and her husband had taken custody of her two kids, Farhad and Farnaz. Farnaz was very young when Nazee left her husband and so she was not very close with Takhanjoon and Afaghjoon and would hardly visit their home. Farhad was older and had a relationship with Nazee before their divorce and would often visit. Farhad was a familiar face every time we visited Tehran and one of the only cousins of mine with whom we spent a lot of time.

My grandparents on baba's side were Babajoon, my grandfather, and Khaleh Badri, my grandmother. Amusingly, Khaleh means aunt in Farsi and so it always confused me as a child that I had to call my grandmother as my aunt. Babajoon and Khaleh Badri had four children, Giti, Mamad, baba, and Hadi. Giti lived with her two sons in Tehran. Amoo Mamad, lived with his wife and two sons in Bandar Abbas and we would often meet them to play video games or spend time together on the beach. Amoo Hadi lived with Babajoon and Khaleh Badri until forty-five, when he, too, married. Interestingly, both maman's and baba's youngest brothers were late bloomers to married life.

Growing up we weren't too close to baba's side of the family. When in Tehran for our vacations, we would live with Takhanjoon and Afaghjoon, and only did day trips to visit Babajoon and Khaleh Badri. I later learned that this was because Khaleh Badri and Giti were never very welcoming of maman, a common cultural behaviour in Iranian families. The women of the groom's family are often socially taught to treat a new bride as competition, something I have deeply resented. But baba would not tolerate this and so intentionally created distance from his family. I always wondered if baba regretted his decision to create this wedge between himself and his parents. I could never imagine breaking the relationship with my parents for the love of any other person.

Summers at Takhanjoon and Afaghjoon's home was the highlight of the year. Their home would have Amoo Farshad, Nazee, Farhad, and my entire family as well. Farhad was the best part of everyone's day. It could be an ordinary Sunday and you run into him at the market, and that would be the most memorable part of your day. It could be a cousin's grand wedding celebration and the 10 minutes you spent with Farhad would be the best part of that celebration. He had a charm and charisma about him. He was witty, funny, and always a treat to be around. If Farhad was going to be there at an event, I would be sure to never miss out! My earliest memories of Farhad go back to when I was five and he was ten, and briefly but distinctly, liking him more than a cousin. He was the first boy that I ever had a crush on. It's weird to think of now, since he was my first cousin. Although Farhad lived in Tehran with his father after the divorce, he was very close and attached to Nazee. He cherished his time with Nazee and would visit our grandparents' home very often to see her, and it is during these visits that our friendship began. Every summer when we would visit Takhanjoon and Afaghjoon's home, Farhad would always be there and spend full weeks with us. Being only a short three-hour flight from Bandar Abbas to Tehran, we would visit maman's family two to three times a year for summers, New Years and other special occasions. And very quickly Farhad would become the best part of every one of those trips. Very often Nazee and my grandparents would come to visit us in Bandar Abbas and Farhad would join them as well. My curiosity had me investigating the reason for Nazee and Farhad's dad's divorce. I would hear bits and pieces of the story from different people. Farhad's paternal grandmother didn't like Nazee, like Khaleh Badri and Giti, and so gave him the ultimatum to either divorce her or be disowned. Being disowned would mean sacrificing his share of his family inheritance, and so his father opted for door number one and divorced the presumed love of his life. For someone that was raised by inseparable parents who were willing to part ways with their own families for the sake of their spouse, I never understood how Farhad's father could so easily leave his wife, and greatly affect his children's lives for the sake of money. I am not sure how true that story is, but later in my life many more events occurred which would solidify my impression of his father being addicted to wealth and possessions. While I would sympathize with the young beggars on the streets of Bandar Abbas, the first time that I truly wanted to better another person's life was that of Farhad. I often wondered if his over-the-top personality was his way of compensating for a lack of a normal childhood and upbringing in a home with two loving parents.

There was a small town just outside of Bandar Abbas called Sari. Amoo Farjad, had a farmhouse with an orchard there and it was his family's vacation home. Lucky for us, Amoo Farjad and his family were always in some far away part of the world and hardly spent a couple of weeks every two years at their farmhouse. This meant that my family were the local guards, and thus inhabitants of their luxurious farmhouse. When Takhanjoon and Afaghjoon would visit us with Nazee and Farhad, we would often spend the week in Sari. We would run through the farms, climb up the fig trees and violently shake the branches to loosen the fruit. Once gathered, we would eat them all until sick to our stomachs, and then play cards until four or five in the morning. We could experience the freedom of wandering freely, and without fear. Our neighbours in Sari would come over as well when they would hear that Farhad was visiting because they wanted to see him and play with him. He was somewhat of a celebrity in our small family and community circle. Being five years older than me and closer to my sister's age, his awareness of my presence was mostly in association with my sister, as Bahar's little sister. He coined my nick name Banooleh that would stick with me for years with Bahar and many other members of maman's extended family.

Farhad was a handsome young boy, with his round face, light skin, and little pointy straight hair. You would always find him dressed well and with a smile on his face. It was no secret he was the boy that all the girls in the neighbourhood had their eye on. Behind that charm and smile was dark pain. Farhad grew up in a home with his father and grandmother constantly spewing horrible anecdotes and characteristics about his mother, Nazee. It must have been a heartbreaking experience to witness the break-up of his parents' marriage at such a young age. I believe he resorted to putting a permanent smile on his face to mask the pain underneath. Iranian culture doesn't have a playbook for young boys and men to deal with negative emotions. The strong machismo and patriarchy driven society frowns upon men who express any other emotions outside of violence and strength. And so, the outlets that men resort to are unhealthy, dangerous, and harmful for their bodies and the people around them. Farhad picked up the habit of smoking before he was even twelve years of age. Casual smoking of cigarettes at twelve combined with lack of a parental support system at home, led him to experiment with much stronger substances as he entered his mid-teens. As he got older, he was obsessed with his physical image and resorted to steroids to achieve the image that he wanted. It was not until I was twenty and returned to Iran that I started to notice these troubling habits.

From Rasht to Hamilton

My family moved from Bandar Abbas to Rasht, a city in the north of Iran, in 1995. Rasht was also a coastal city on the Caspian Sea and known as the "City of Rain". Baba had a job as an interpreter primarily translating immigration documents from Farsi to English for Iranians applying for immigration to western countries. After hundreds of translations, he came home one day and asked maman and us a question that had been gnawing at him for months.

"Why don't we leave Iran and move to the West?".

Iranians often immigrated to Australia, the USA, and Canada. With Amoo Farjad being in Vancouver, and having several personal friends in Canada, and being aware of the large Iranian communities present in most major cities in Canada, the selection of the country was obvious.

It was a long two-year process that included tens of applications, nightly family discussions, handfuls of medical examinations, and a lot of celebrations at the completion of every milestone. These were two of the best years of my life. As soon as we submitted the first round of applications, our friends and family from all over Iran, began to visit. The visa could appear at any moment, and so we might not have enough time for the customary goodbyes. Our community in Rasht held celebrations after every cleared step in the immigration process. There was a big street potluck after we heard the interview was successful and a 'Canada' themed costume party after the clearance of the medical examinations. The two years felt like one giant party, I was allowed to sleep late every night and ignore school and homework, since we would be leaving the country very shortly. The community of Rasht became family to my parents. Baba never forgot this community's love and could never replicate it anywhere else, and twenty years later he would return to Rasht to enjoy his retirement.

In my last year in Iran, I got accepted into a prestigious school and their gifted program. I wasn't sure why my parents were still setting such high educational aspirations for us in Iran when everything seemed so temporary. This elementary school was every Rasht parents' dream for their child as it almost guaranteed an admission into the best secondary schools, and from there the best colleges in Iran. But, as an eleven-year-old, my future went only as far as which TV shows I would be watching that evening. To me, getting admitted to this school meant only a lot of homework and assignments, which would occupy precious time that I wanted to spend watching Shah Rukh Khan in a Bollywood movie. I thought it would be amusing to spend my efforts mouthing off to my teachers, getting in trouble, and spending time in the principal's office. Since this was not a school owned and operated by baba, unlike in Bandar Abbas, I didn't fear ruining my parent's reputation. One warm day in May, when my peers were scrambling and stressing about final exams, I decided to take a stand and not wear the school uniform that day. So, instead I went to school in jeans. I persuaded my parents, somehow, and as expected I was immediately sent to the Principal's office. My unfortunate parents were called to discuss my recent, and repetitive, rebellious behaviour. To my absolute surprise, before the principal could even start speaking, baba said "Banafsheh is leaving this school". There was nothing else to discuss, it was the last day of my schooling in Iran.

Although baba had pulled me out of school on that warm day in May, we wouldn't leave Iran for four more months, not until our visas appeared on a bright September day. With each passing week, Baba had stayed optimistic and confident that we would get our visas "any day now". Visits to our community mailbox now happened twice a day, even though the mail only arrived once a day.

As Maman had a master's in Mechanical Engineering, it made her the more suitable primary applicant for our visas. She was determined to enhance our application and maximize our overall points on the application, by learning French. She hired a tutor to teach her the language and had achieved conversational fluency before even the arrival of our visa. We were so sure that our visa was 'just around the corner' that baba and maman started to sell our household belongings hoping not to leave all the packing and planning until the very end. Everything that they had ever owned and accumulated was being sold – furniture, clothes, and our library filled with books. So many books! Baba would stamp every book he owned with his name.

So, after a local store came in and purchased all our books, when they were later resold, they would appear in the homes of other members of the community knowing that this treasure originally came from M. Karbalaei's library. After my siblings and I were pulled out of school, my parents quit their jobs, sold all our belongings, and the endless waiting began.

With every passing week, baba started to grow suspicious that something was going on in the visa office. Finally, tired of waiting and running out of patience, one day in September, he decided to personally pay a visit to the visa office to inquire about the status of our application. When he arrived at the counter, seeing the agent behind the desk, he decided to take his chances. That morning maman had made him realize that he might have to tackle this visa delay issue in a more traditional Iranian way. So, he packed two envelopes and strategically decided to fill one with some bribe money and the other one with a desperate letter pleading for their visa to be processed. When he got to the counter, face-to-face with the agent behind the desk, his instincts told him to use envelope number one. The agent opened the envelope, slowly got out of his chair, went into cabinet behind his desk, casually retrieved our visas, and handed it to baba. They did not exchange any other words. No one will ever know how long that visa had been waiting, collecting dust, in that cabinet drawer. Two weeks later, we were boarding an Aeroflot flight to Moscow, and then the final connection to Toronto.

Bahar was twenty, I was twelve, and Kasra was six as we stepped out on to Canadian soil. I didn't speak a word of English. Immigrating to Canada, for baba and maman, was only for one reason – to open every possible door of opportunity for Bahar, Kasra and myself. On our first leg of the trip to Moscow, after we settled in and the wheels were off the ground, maman asked Bahar and I to take off our head coverings. This felt strange because we had never done this in public before. Looking back, there could not have been anything more symbolic to gesture the separation from our past in Iran and the opportunities that were waiting in our future in Canada. After we would remove our head coverings, mama would tell us that we never have to wear it again. I knew at that very moment, a new chapter in my life was beginning.

We landed in Canada on Friday September 24th, 1999, just months from the turn of the millennium.

We were picked up at Toronto's Pearson airport by my parent's friends, who welcomed us in to their small three-bedroom apartment in the north end of Hamilton, a smaller city outside of Toronto.

The north end of Hamilton, especially in 1999, was not a part of town that you wanted to be wandering in past sunset. But to my innocent eyes, this neighbourhood seemed like every Farsi-dubbed-American-movie that we had watched in Iran. Everything was urban, convenient, and consistent. Large stores, like Walmart, sold a variety of breads perfectly packaged in plastic, like they had come off a conveyor belt. In Iran, I was used to purchasing bread from small bakeries, with minor differences in shape, hand wrapped in newspaper upon purchase.

Everything felt foreign, intriguing, and worthy of a comparison to its counterpart back home. We landed on a Friday, and my parents had enrolled us in school by the following Monday. The four months of sleeping in and no homework had come to a screeching halt. We would take the same lunch to school every day, which consisted of a cold meat and plain white Wonder Bread sandwich and a small Coke. Approximately two weeks after we had arrived, my parents were able to rent an apartment in the same complex as their friends. We excitedly moved into our new home with the ten checked-in bags of belongings we had so thoughtfully packed and brought from Iran.

I started school on September 27th not knowing more than nine or ten words in English. I was enrolled in ESL classes immediately for one hour per day. On the first day of school, as baba and I met my new principal together, baba reminded me of the last time that I was in the principal's office on the last day of school in Iran. I promised to be better here. My school principal couldn't say my name, Banafsheh. He struggled for a minute trying all variations – Baufashi, Banafashu, and many other combinations of sounds that were utterly butchering my name. And finally, baba interrupted and said, "you can call her Violet", the English translation of my beautiful Farsi name that I loved. And over twenty years later, I'm still Violet.

The first six months were very challenging for me and my teachers, as they didn't know how to educate me with such a huge language barrier. I would come home to ask baba and maman how to say sentences in English so that I could return the next day and ask them my questions. Every experience felt new and as if I was in a movie. After six months of challenges and struggles with my ESL class, I was finally getting a hold of the English language. In ten months, I became comfortable communicating my thoughts to my peers and my teachers and being able to fully comprehend what they were saying. In fourteen months, I was better at the English language than my peers. To this day, my spelling is excellent, and I owe that entirely to all the TV shows that I would watch when we first arrived in Canada. The closed captioning, in English, managed to teach me a lot more than my ESL teachers.

F*CK Cancer

That six-letter word that everyone unanimously hates, cancer, was getting ready to creep into my life and consume every aspect of it. It's like the smoke from a burning room entering the adjacent space, through every tiny crack and opening, even though the door is closed and its welcome unwanted. I was sixteen years old when my parents called me into their bedroom one evening. Maman began this long story about the Iranian revolution, the two sides involved, and minute details that were of little interest to me. I had just wanted to spend the last couple of hours of the evening watching some TV. She told me about the Shah, at the time, being diagnosed with prostate cancer. She then explained how science had come such a long way since those days, and there was now a cure for prostate cancer. This long, drawn out story came to an abrupt, climactic end as she explained to me that baba was just diagnosed with prostate cancer. I remember being shocked and confused like watching a movie with a highly complex storyline. I wanted to pause that conversation on my parents' bed, but maman continued and confidently explained that baba was going to get the necessary treatment and would be just fine. I was used to this side of maman where she would control the narrative in stressful situations, and her sense of control would put my entire family at ease. Defying patriarchal convention, she was our family's fearless leader.

Baba was quickly setup with the necessary appointments, and within a few weeks, went into surgery at St. Joseph's hospital in Hamilton. It was a long surgery, almost twelve hours. I remember the doctors being so proud when they came out of the operating room to update us. Although it had been a difficult surgery, it was a successful one. Their tired but faint smiles was enough for me to immediately pick up that everything was well, and that baba was going to be okay. Maman wasn't working at that time and baba had a variety of part-time jobs which he had to quit. We didn't have any income during baba's surgery and recovery period. We thanked our lucky stars that we were in Canada, where all the expensive medical procedures, treatments, and medications would be covered by the public healthcare system. They had innocently discovered the cancer, in its early stages, during one of baba's routine physical examinations. Now, just a couple of months after the initial diagnosis, he was in recovery.

The celebration for baba's recovery was hardly over, and as was our nightly custom sitting on our parents' bed and reminiscing, we were all in our usual arrangement listening to Kasra recite the events at his school that day. My parents' bedroom was like a second living room for us. We would gather on their bed and chat for hours after lunch, on weekend afternoons, or even before going to bed. Maman always had an entertaining story to share about something she watched on TV or that she had heard from the neighbours. One day, as she was storytelling, her speech suddenly started to change.

The words coming out of her mouth weren't making any sense, they were gibberish. Able to hear her own speech, she quickly realized what was happening, and immediately fell silent. Fear, like I had never seen before, not even when our home was burgled in Bandar Abbas all those years ago, overwhelmed her face. Baba immediately comforted her, asked us all to leave because she was tired, and told us that it was time to go to bed. I wonder if baba knew that night would be one of the last peaceful nights with his wife.

Women in maman's family have always struggled with a little bit of extra weight, heart disease, and hypertension. Maman always monitored her blood pressure, having seen other family members suffer from uncontrolled hypertension. But these symptoms were entirely unusual to both of my parents. Maman couldn't sleep all night and at the crack of dawn my parents were off to the ER and the diagnosis came back as pre-stroke symptoms, which to our non-scientific exposure made sense. She was prescribed a strict, daily rehabilitation program at a stroke clinic for one month. Just like baba's cancer, we thanked our lucky stars once again to have discovered the problem early on and had placed complete trust in the Canadian healthcare system for maman's recovery.

Having just recovered from prostate cancer, baba continued to have frequent check-ins with our family doctor. Dr. Kumaisril, from the day we signed up at his clinic has loved my family, always engaging in longer sessions than permitted by the medical billing system and inquiring about our adjustments and integration into Canadian life. Although this appointment was for baba, it was during maman's one-month rehab period, and he inquired about maman's health. He had seen her reports that were sent to him from the ER with the details of her stroke. When he found out from baba that maman was not sent in for an MRI, or any type of a brain scan, he shook his head in disappointment and immediately sent in a requisition. A couple of days later, maman was lying on an MRI bed and on the following day, which happened to be Mother's Day, we received the MRI report, which stated a diagnosis that maman had Glioblastoma.

Glioblastoma is an aggressive form of brain cancer. It's the same cancer that killed Gord Downie from the Tragically Hip and the United States Republican senator and navy veteran John McCain. It's brutal, violent, and completely unforgiving. If you are diagnosed with this tumour, you are given a 5%

chance of survival for five years after and a 50% chance of making it through the first year. I would learn more about probability and statistics in the upcoming months than in any other high school or university course. All that medical jargon on the MRI report translated into the fact that maman had a baseball sized tumour in her brain.

To this day, I question who suffers more while taking care of a loved one who is battling an aggressive disease with very unpromising odds. The upcoming months were the darkest days of my perfect family's life. The treatment plan started immediately with hospital visits, surgeon consults, oncologist appointments and on and on. Maman was our rock, she was the leader of our pack. She took control whenever our family faced a challenge. It was second nature for all of us, including baba, to turn to her for guidance in difficult situations. And so, when our captain was falling, it felt like our entire ship was sinking. Baba couldn't even find the courage to tell us of the three-month prognosis that she had received from the doctors. He just left the note out on the kitchen table for us to read on our own and process the information in our individual minds. We never spoke about it.

The real shock hit us when we saw what the disease had done to maman. Like a magician that snaps his fingers and the bird in the cage disappears, maman withdrew so quickly in the blink of an eye. She was terrified of what was going to happen to her incomplete life and it filled and drowned the rest of us in fear. She did not tell anyone in our social circles about her illness. Immediately after her diagnosis, we had gone for a friend's daughter's bridal shower where her best friends were all there. Maman sat at the corner of the room and hardly spoke to anyone, an unimaginable version of maman that her friends could not understand. Maman was the life of every party and this behaviour of hers was frightening for all the guests in attendance. Maman felt that if she did not tell people about her tumour that it wouldn't be this real and scary thing. She was not ready to open the closet doors and let out the monster.

Two months after the diagnosis, she went in for her first surgery which took hours to complete, and it felt like we were in the waiting room for days on end waiting for the doctors to come out of the operating room. I was eagerly waiting to see that familiar tired but faint smile. That was my indication and comfort that everything was going to be okay. The doctors finally emerged into the waiting room with unrecognizable looks as my family stood up quickly and excitedly to hear the outcome. "It was invasive and aggressive", the doctor said, "and we were able to remove some parts of the mass and relieved some of the pressure in her brain". We did not know what that meant. Was maman going to survive? The hospital requested the chaplain to come and visit us in maman's room to help us prepare our goodbyes. This wonderful chaplain was there to help us with our prayers as we were probably going to lose her that night. We were never a religious family. Although being Muslim by birth, land, and name, we weren't a family that said prayers or attended religious events. Saying a prayer for baba or any of us was as foreign an activity as skiing or ballet or anything like that which we had seen others do and watched on television but wouldn't dare attempt.

And in these final moments with maman, I couldn't believe I had to rely on something so foreign to connect me to her. So, all I could say sitting beside maman in that semi-private hospital room was "please don't die, please don't die, please don't die," over and over again. I couldn't even look at baba because he was crying uncontrollably. Bahar and I stayed that night in the hospital while baba took Kasra back home. I still remember the kind faces of all the nurses who helped my sister and I that night. When I think back to that night, theirs are the kind faces that come to my mind. I didn't sleep that night, not for one minute. I just stared at maman's chest to make sure it went up and down with every breath. I would give maman small goals to achieve- just keep breathing until 2 am. When she would achieve that the goal, the post would then move to 3 am. This continued until the sun came up and her chest was still going up and down. The doctors couldn't believe this, and shortly after, her recovery and transition into St. Peter's palliative care unit began. We were going to have maman around for a little while longer.

It was almost exactly eight months after the Glioblastoma diagnosis, on that crisp and sunny Mother's Day that maman took her last breath. I remember it like yesterday. It was November 20th, 2004. Kasra had turned twelve on November 18th, and I was in my first semester for grade twelve, thinking of post-secondary education and starting their applications. It was a Saturday night, and baba had taken Kasra out for a movie to celebrate his birthday. Maman was typically the parent that made all the fuss around our birthdays to make it a very special day for us. With maman in palliative care and unable to do this anymore, it was important for baba to continue to provide Kasra, who was such a young boy, all the normalcy that he deserved. Bahar was at work, and I was home alone. St. Peter's hospital, where maman had been in palliative care, called to talk to baba. They said that maman was breathing abnormally. I asked if I needed to come down to the hospital or rather if I should, but they wouldn't divulge any further information since I was seventeen and still considered a minor. They just said, "let your dad know to give us a call as soon as he is back". I knew baba's phone would be on silent as he forced his laughs along with Kasra's to Sponge Bob Square Pants, all the while just counting down the minutes until he could be by maman's side again. And my sister was not answering her phone either, which was not surprising as she was working a night shift as a nurse. I had a feeling something was very wrong with maman and so I called a taxi to go to the hospital. Just before I left our home, my uncle in Vancouver had called our landline and I told him the news which led him to drive straight to the airport and he got on the next flight to Toronto. I got out of the taxi and rushed inside the hospital to maman's room dodging nurses walking patients in the hallway and meal carts tucked away outside the patient rooms waiting to be picked up by housekeeping. In all the panic and rush to make it to maman's room, I knew the goal was just to see her chest move up and down, which was my confirmation that she was breathing and alive. Out of breath and hardly breathing myself I ran into maman's room, and locked eyes directly with her chest for one second, two seconds, three seconds, four seconds. It didn't move. Time had stopped. Maman wasn't breathing, she was gone. The nurse ran behind me and started to say, "I'm sorry, I'm sorry". I didn't cry all night. I didn't have a cellphone with stored phone numbers and only had my sister's phone number memorized and so I kept calling her, but she wasn't answering. The nurses offered to continue to call her so that I could sit by maman's side.

My parents had celebrated their thirtieth and last anniversary together in the hospital. I saved a thousand dollars from my part time job and bought a diamond ring for maman. It was the tiniest diamond. Her hands and fingers were so swollen from all the medications that it needed resizing for an extra two hundred dollars. Baba presented the ring to maman for their anniversary. It would be the one and only diamond that maman ever got in her life.

I had left a note for baba at our front door in Farsi and English – "Hospital called; I'm headed there". He knew. Baba and Kasra didn't even take their jackets off when they returned from the movie, they turned right around, and called a taxi. The taxi driver asked them where they were going and my innocent eleven-year-old brother replied, "We are going to see my mom, I think she just died". Baba started having panic attacks when he saw maman just lying there, the nurses had to medicate him to calm him down. The last two months before maman passed were bare and ripped and filled with unhappiness. Baba would go to work and spend every evening at the hospital, while my siblings and I went to work and school. We would all return late in the evening and Baba, Bahar and I would silently drink tequila and then go to sleep and do it all over again the next day. I wished I could trade all the money in my bank and all my future happiness to just get maman's health back and be back with my family on the beaches of Bandar Abbas searching for clams. The glioblastoma had sucked all life and laughter out of my family.

Maman's battle with cancer and subsequent death made me see the best and worst sides of people. My friends Candace and Linda were seventeen-year-old, high school kids that would prepare and bring me food, take me to the hospital, talk with me for hours on msn messenger, and were by my side the entire time. I will never be able to pay them back for their love and support. The Iranian community of Hamilton brought us food every day. These were all immigrant families like ours that didn't have too many resources, but they gave everything that they had to take care of my family and I am forever indebted to them. It was as if all those years of maman listening to the concerns of others in her community, rallying for worker's rights, putting others before herself, was all delivered back into my family's life, ten fold, with their love and support. My peers and teachers, at school were no different in their kindness and understanding. I was a smart, polite, and energetic student with a lot of passion about education, but without much enthusiasm for schoolwork. I was the president of the graduation committee, part of the history group, and involved in many extra curriculars, but all my assignments were handed in late. There was just one teacher and one class that I wanted to get out of. He was racist, and I had heard him tell one of my Iraqi classmates to go back to Iraq. I begged and pleaded with my principal one afternoon to get me out of that class. And he surprised me as he said, "Sure Violet, why don't you start in room 214 tomorrow and let Ms. Mandolia know that I sent you". Ms. Mandolia was the rainbow in my clouds. This was a self-paced class with students of diverse background like kids from foster home situations, and even a few others who were out of juvenile prison, and me, whose mother had just died of an aggressive cancer. In that room I met the most supportive group of peers and learnt some of the hardest English.

Being a senior at the precipice of high school graduation, and having just lost her mother, I was a bit distracted and missed all the signs of baba falling apart. Baba flew to Iran to have a wake for maman and was gone for two months. My siblings and I spent Christmas and the holidays alone that year. We were at the movie theatre one day during the

Christmas break, when my sister, out of the blue, told me how you can marry people from abroad and bring them to Canada. She specifically referenced maman's sister and my favourite aunt, Nazee. It was 2004, one year after the Canadian supreme court had legalized same-sex marriages and I thought my sister was going to marry my aunt. It was the strangest conversation that we were having at the local theatre waiting in line for popcorn, but I had no idea that what she was preparing me for was to be even more strange. My sister then told me that baba was going to marry Nazee and bring her to Canada.

My head and world started to spin. It was the exact same confused feeling I had felt when maman had told us about baba's prostate cancer. Why now? Why is this the time to do something like this? I knew that maman had tried for years to sponsor Nazee and her two children, my cousins Farhad and Farnaz, to immigrate to Canada. During high school I worked part-time at an immigration law office and used some of my networks from the firm to write to my local MPs appealing to the government to issue a "compassionate visa" for Nazee to visit her sister during maman's last few months. But all our efforts were in vain. And now baba was going to marry her? How could baba do this to the love of his life just a couple of months after her passing? Baba called us one day from Iran and asked to speak to me on the phone. It's as if he knew that I was the one that was putting up the biggest resistance to this. He phrased the sentence in a ceremonious Farsi manner to say, "with your permission, Banoojan, I would like to marry Nazee". For just a moment, I wished I had died with maman the month before. Baba knew Nazee since they were teenagers, and she was his deceased wife's younger sister and now going to become his new wife.

Baba returned to Canada a few months later with a little bit of maman's insurance inheritance which he put towards a small townhome that we purchased in Hamilton. Kasra started high school that fall of 2005, I started at McMaster University and things were starting to feel like normal again. And then immediately after maman's first death anniversary, in December of 2005, Nazee arrived in Canada as baba's wife with her daughter and my cousin Farnaz, now also my stepsister. Growing up in Iran, I was only close to Farhad because of all the time he would spend with us during our vacations. Farnaz was very young when Nazee and their father divorced and would hardly visit our grand parents' home in

Tehran. I liked Farnaz, but I didn't know her enough. I loved my aunt Nazee but wanted her to remain only as my aunt. But now they were my stepmom and my stepsister and had moved into our newly purchased home and Nazee had moved in with baba into what should have been maman's room. We never gathered on their bed for late night chats and daily catchups. As for Farhad, I would reminisce my fond childhood memories with him and I didn't mind our new relationship as much, and I wondered when he would be able to join Nazee and Farnaz in Canada. Since he was over eighteen and considered an adult, he was not eligible for the dependent status visa into Canada.

It had been a year since that day in St. Peter's hospital when I said goodbye to the strongest woman that I would ever know. When I would ask maman who her favourite person was, expecting the answer to be me, she would always tell me that baba was her favourite person since she had chosen him as her partner, while I was brought in to her life with pre-determined characteristics. But what I never told maman, in return, was that she was my favourite person in the whole world.

Blended Family

When they moved to Canada, Farnaz was twenty-one and so felt closer in age to Bahar who was also in her twenties. Together they would be more interested in the cultural Iranian community based activities such as meeting other Iranians of their age, while I had close Canadian high school friends and a social life outside of my Iranian culture which I was more invested and interested in. But it didn't take long for Farnaz and I to become close and for me to trust her like a sister. Nazee and I, unfortunately, would take much longer to understand each other and it felt like our pre-existing relationship of an aunt and niece was eroding in a forced effort to establish ourselves as stepmom and stepdaughter. I was mostly to blame for the duration of time it was taking to build our new relationship. I felt betrayed by baba, and by my siblings that had replaced maman so easily by growing fond of Nazee. My loyalty towards maman remained inspired by my childhood books that taught love for one's country and the noble acts of kings and queens; and this meant not accepting Nazee as baba's new wife. Understanding maman's character with more maturity today, this combative behaviour that I expressed towards Nazee is in exact opposition of what maman would have wanted from me. But that wisdom would not come to me until a lot later.

I turned and focused all my attention into my university education. It was going to be my new chapter. Away from the past of my dying mother, and my forced new family relationships, McMaster University was going to create a new life and reality for me. I was going to debate with my classmates about every subject, and we were going to change the world with our bachelor's degrees in social sciences. So, it came as a complete shock to me when nothing about University inspired me. After the last two years of receiving shocking news one after another like baba's prostate cancer, maman's glioblastoma, and baba's new wife, I thought I was well equipped for surprise discoveries and that nothing could startle me any longer. But I didn't see this coming. My courses were boring. My professors were stale and severely lacked inspiration. My classmates were not whom I expected. This complete shift in expectations compounded with my inability to express any of this to my new family sent me down a spiraling path of craving maman's presence and her guidance more than ever before. I started struggling with anxiety and mild forms of depression. We were six grown adults under one small roof. I started to live my life in a bubble. I forcefully attended my classes, where I would sit alone and keep my head down. I was a quiet and unenthusiastic employee at my part-time job. And when I got home, I would lock myself in my room and watch TV on my computer, only briefly exiting my room to grab food or go to the bathroom. I kept up with this routine until the end of my first year in April of 2006, which is when I decided to drop out of University. It created huge waves of tension at home, especially with baba. Our home, once the place of great laughter on maman and baba's bed, turned into a brewing ground of confusion, miscommunication, and judgement. Every night after Baba and Kasra would go to bed, the four women of the home would inevitably gravitate into some heated discussion. Thinking back at those days, I can't even remember the details of any of our fights. They were childish quarrels where no one was willing to see the other side and everyone got defensive and offended too quickly. My aloof, unwelcoming behaviour and I'm-Canadian-and-can't-relate-to-your-Iranian-ways self was not helping ease any of that tension. Baba and Bahar worked full-time, and I worked part-time during this period. Baba's salary alone could not pay for all our home expenses and so he asked for Bahar and I to start chipping in. And that would lay the groundwork for so many of my frustrations with Nazee, asking very passive aggressively why she couldn't work and become a contributing member of this family? Because maman would have.

Once I quit university and since I only worked part-time, I started to be home more often than I would have liked but my bubble of staying in my room continued. And in my short movements from my room to the bathroom or to the kitchen I would hear Nazee talk to Baba or others about her son and my cousin, Farhad. I would eavesdrop and hear her on the phone with him almost daily repeating how much she missed him. Having lived in Canada for seven years now, and never returned to visit Iran, my memories of Farhad were fading to mere sensational memories of laughing a lot when around him and not so much concrete and factual experiences that we shared together. It felt like Nazee's emotions would heighten and be exaggerated every time I was outside in the hallway more so than when I was locked in my room, as if she really wanted for me to witness her turmoil more than anyone else. She would tell baba how Farhad is taking their marriage with such difficulty because in the Iranian culture there is an unspoken ownership of adult sons over their mothers. Everyone felt so empathetic and sorry for this wonderful young man whom they so desperately wanted to bring to Canada for a better life. But all these same individuals knew very well that Farhad was far from this idyllic Iranian son and gentleman. Farhad struggled with drugs most of his adult life and from putting pieces of the conversations together in my head, that struggle was still ongoing. Everyone in the house seemed to agree that the right thing to do was to bring Farhad to Canada and that somehow being on Canadian soil and smelling the breeze that travelled from the great lakes was the cure for the decade long lifestyle of addiction that he endured. Since he was over the dependent age when Nazee and Farnaz immigrated, he was not granted a visa by the Canadian government.

Through the Iranian community rumour mill, Nazee heard that if they paid forty to fifty thousand dollars to a willing Canadian girl, she would go to Iran, stage an entire wedding celebration, legally marry the boy in need of a visa, and bring him to Canada as her spouse. And once he was in Canada, they would mutually agree to a divorce. I laughed at these schemes that I would hear Nazee and Farnaz discuss as I walked between my bedroom and the kitchen. I wanted to inform them that they had watched too many Bollywood movies which had persuaded them of this possibility. They were naïve to the independence and education that Canadian women were bestowed with that didn't make them desperate enough to resort to such measures to earn a living. With each passing day, these discussions of visa schemes would increase in seriousness as would my indifference and quarrels with Nazee. I hated that baba would have to get in between us to resolve our differences and that my stubbornness was saddening the man who loved and treated me with the utmost respect for my entire life. And then one evening, I decided on my way from the kitchen back into my room that I would sit on the L-sectional couch in our family room and join the conversation with my family. Nazee, without fail, was talking about Farhad and how much she wished he was here with all of us.

I have replayed this very moment in my head many times, but the details of the events that followed are always blurred. I don't remember being asked any questions, I don't recall anyone requesting my opinion about the matter. The only thing I can remember is saying out loud what I was sure was only in my head, until it wasn't.

"What if I marry Farhad?".

It was less than two seconds. A consequence of me never practicing the concept of 'think before you speak'. Was it even my decision? Could months of listening to a sad mother missing her son have subconsciously implanted this idea in my head? What did everyone respond with? Was it final and decided, am I getting married? To this day, still a blur.

Baba was driving me to the mall the next day and for the first time since I had dropped out of University, did I see a smile on his kind face. He kept re-iterating how happy he was that I had decided to help my cousin in this way. Nazee couldn't thank me enough and like a simple light switch the differences in our relationship had turned off. Nazee's gratitude towards my decision was daily and even hourly sometimes, phrased and rephrased in Farsi and English and in any other gesture that she could offer. Never did anyone ask me "Are you sure, Banoo?" or "Do you want to discuss it further before making such a huge life decision?" Their surprise at my idea of marrying Farhad seemed disingenuous but all their gratitude felt sincere. So, I removed the thoughts of manipulation out of my head and held on to the feeling of sincere gratitude. The government of

Canada, rightfully so, required large amounts of proof of a spousal relationship including phone logs, pictures from before, during, and after the wedding, records of the couple dating, and many other requirements. And with this began a fully orchestrated operation of curating my love for my cousin, Farhad, my engagement to him, and a full throttle planning of my big fat Iranian wedding to my stepbrother.

Return to Tehran

The plan was set for me to go back to Iran with Farnaz for 3 weeks. We would organize the wedding during the first two weeks, sign the papers, take the necessary pictures, and return to Canada a few days after the wedding. We left Toronto on March 10th, 2007. It was 10 days before Nowruz, which is the Iranian new year. Baba managed to get us last minute tickets to Tehran with a stopover at the Amsterdam Schiphol Airport. This was my first visit back to Iran since my family immigrated to Canada. The last time that I was in Iran, maman was alive, Nazee was still only my aunt and I was a twelve-year-old without a care in the world and definitely not contemplating an impending marriage to my stepbrother. The entire seven-hour flight to Iran I reminisced about that simpler life which seemed like a faint memory that I wouldn't even recognize if it came right up and starred me in the face. We wisely decided to spend the entire eight-hour layover at the bar for two reasons. Firstly, Heinekens were cheaper than water, and secondly because drinking in public spaces was prohibited in Iran and this seemed like a good way to squeeze in one last social drinking at a bar experience. Farnaz and I were never very close like you would expect siblings living under the same roof to be, but one can never underestimate what eight hours of drinking together can do for a relationship.

By the time we were boarding our flight from Amsterdam to Tehran, we were ready to add a third layer to our relationship status, first cousins, then stepsisters, and now soon to be in-laws.

We landed in Tehran and were picked up by Farhad and Farnaz's dad and driven to their home in a part of the city that I had never visited before. They lived in a small apartment building in a crowded and trendy neighbourhood of Tehran. Leading up to the apartment on the small side street were lines of shops that sold clothes, shoes, vegetables, and a variety of other assorted goods. It was a fraction of the size of the bazaars of Bandar Abbas but sitting in the back seat of the taxi with Farnaz immediately transposed my mind to the days when I would jump into the back of baba's blue Chevy as we drove into the bazaar to buy something. A small smile returned to my face grateful that my fond childhood memories were not lost forever like I thought, but I was physically aching to have baba and maman next to me. The first-floor apartment was where Farhad, his dad and his stepmom lived. And the upstairs apartment, which was owned by their grandmother, was graciously given to Farnaz and I to share privately so that we could enjoy the space and separation from the others. Entering the apartment and dropping off my suitcase, I immediately felt homesick and anxiety as I missed baba and was somewhat confused that he didn't accompany me to support me during my wedding. In the hurry of organizing the plane ticket and packing my suitcases, I never got the chance to ask him that question in person. I never grew up in Tehran and so didn't have too many associations or memories to the capital city. Bombarded with decisions about the wedding and questions about my likes and dislikes for the ceremony had me completely burnt out and in a hurry, just two days before Nowruz, I decided to leave and go to Rasht to visit Bahar's best friend. Maman and baba always preached the importance of friends being like your chosen family and they spent countless time and resources to help their friends and neighbours like they would their own blood relatives. Friends of the family were like family to me, and so Bahar's best friend was like a pseudo sister to me and retrieving to her family's home in the midst of the wedding planning chaos was the closest thing to being with family.

Farhad's stepmom was a lovely lady. I would always overhear Nazee comment on how she was so happy that her son was being raised by such a wonderful woman, albeit she was sad it was not herself. It was strange for me to be interacting with Farnaz's dad and even more strange to live in his home because growing up, I hardly saw or knew him. Everything that I heard about him was from maman's side of the family, and they were mostly about his thirst for wealth and possessions and his ability to destroy every person and relationship that came in between him and this greed. He was the antagonist in all our lives, starting with when he divorced Nazee to secure his family inheritance. I always imagined him like Smeagol, even physically, from the Lord of the Rings who ruined every good thing in his life for the pursuit of the One Ring and it's power. And now to be in his home with his hospitality and planning a wedding with his kind wife, made me question the stories and anecdotes shared with me over the years about him. Farhad's step-mom was a very resourceful woman in

Tehran who always knew someone that knew someone that could get anything done around the city that you wanted, which for a person planning a wedding was exactly the person you wanted by your side. She setup appointments for me at the best dress stores and makeup parlours and organized all the minutia details needed to convince the Canadian government of my honest love for my cousin and our legitimate wedding. But as we got closer to the scheduled date, it became evident that even planning a make-believe wedding in less than two weeks was near impossible. And with that my 3-week wedding vacation in Iran transitioned into a 3 month stay.

This extension proved to be a blessing in disguise. Baba instinctively knew that I would need him if I was going to be in Iran for an extended period, and immediately booked a flight and landed in Tehran.

Because of the breathing room that the extension had given us all, the wedding planning quickly transitioned into an enjoyable interruption to a day filled with family visits instead of a chore that needed attention 24/7. I connected with old friends and relatives from Bandar Abbas, Rasht, Tehran, and other parts of Iran. I visited so many of the incredible people that made my childhood years in Iran so enjoyable. I spend hours with people that knew maman intimately, and spent hours listening to them recite stories and memories of the legend that I always knew she was. I craved more information about maman and travelled to various parts of the country to hear from more of her friends and family, so that I could understand maman more deeply and fully. It was in the thick of my teenage years that maman was diagnosed and it was a deep regret of mine that I didn't take the time during those years to learn more from her.

I loved Iran as a child and couldn't be happier to be celebrating my twentieth birthday here, something I was entirely against prior to leaving Canada. It was one of the main conditions that I promised baba to keep for me, which was to bring me back to Canada before my birthday so that I could enter the next decade of my life with my Canadian friends. That was the case no more. My love for this country and it's cultures which I had shoved away in the dark corners of my closet along with my head covering and my real name, erupted out of that dark corner. I had forgotten how much I loved my name, and hearing friends in Iran call me Banafsheh made me smile every time. All my family and friends travelled and celebrated this milestone birthday with me in

Rasht. Farhad and Farnaz came as well and it felt like I was twelve years old again and at one of maman's birthday parties for me, complete with all my favourite foods, decorations, and people. Wedding planning in Iran now seemed like an excuse for what was slowly turning into Violet converting back into Banafsheh and falling back in love with Iran.

I know of several friends that have always planned every detail about their wedding from a very young age. What kind of dress they wanted to wear, the type of ring they would have their fiancé's purchase, their hairdo, and every other last bit of detail. But for me, the wedding day bore no significance. Baba and maman had the perfect marriage and that marriage was something that I always dreamt of, but hardly the wedding just like they didn't and had got married in an inconspicuous ceremony with close family and friends in maman's parents' home. Deep down in my subconscious I equated a small and meaningful wedding to be a leading indicator for a long and fruitful marriage. My lack of interest in the colour theme for the wedding or the floral arrangements turned into points of contention between me and Farhad's stepmom. Meanwhile the bigger and more important traditional and cultural conflicts that I cared about were silly and didn't warrant a conversation by anyone. For example, there is a "Sugar Rubbing" ceremony as part of Iranian weddings where close family will hold a veil over the couple's heads and rub pieces of sugar over it so small flakes fall on to them to symbolize wishing them a very sweet marriage together and it is traditionally the single women in the family that rub the sugar over the couple's heads. Superstitiously this act is supposed to bring good luck to them so they may get married soon. Centuries of patriarchy have embedded similar kinds of traditions into weddings in all ethnic groups including the western culture and the throwing of the bouquet. I always struggled with these traditions and why young women in all cultures were taught this inherent need to get married as if it's the only goal a young woman should strive towards? My defense and reasoning to not want to include these ceremonies in my wedding was because I would think of how I was going to explain to the immigration officer in Canada this very sexist tradition. Never mind the legal and financial responsibility that I was undertaking by marrying someone and bringing them as my dependent into Canada. And never mind if this person then committed a crime or couldn't find a job or got into some other kind of trouble and I was legally and financially responsible for them by signing that marriage certificate.

When I had agreed to marry Farhad, I was in a bad place. I had lost my hero to an aggressive cancer, I had quit university which was something I was looking forward to my entire life so that I could be just like maman with her stacked resume of having a master's in Mechanical Engineering, my family dynamic had entirely changed and I felt like conflicted as an adult that should be contributing more to society. Marrying Farhad, somewhere deep down, was an attempt to validate my existence, to contribute by making people happy again, making Nazee reunite with her son, and playing a hand in bettering the life of a young man who was a victim of substance abuse. I convinced myself that if I could marry Farhad and make Nazee happy and Farnaz reconnected with her brother, I would have been of service to someone.

As we got closer to the date of the wedding the small details started infuriating me. Out of the blue, I was concerned about the sleeves on my dress, or the lack there of. Everyone around me insisted on getting a body wax and I vehemently refused.

"I had agreed to giving him my signature and that was all", is what I would scream out. "My body hair remains exactly where it is".

"I do"

A lot of things transpired in the three and a half months that we were in Iran. Farnaz started dating a guy that she would continue the relationship from Canada for the next five to six years. I rejuvenated old connections, and made a ton of new friends, something that I was unable to do at University. Iran revived my confidence in myself. During my travels between Tehran and Rasht, Farhad would often join. But when we would be in Rasht, he would disappear for a few days in a row. I was so engrossed in my renewed Banafsheh identity, that I would hardly notice or care to read between the lines. Even family members would notice his disappearance, but nobody acknowledged or spoke about and it was better to sweep under the rug. Everyone preferred to hang on to their childhood memories of Farhad, that charming, funny, loving kid who was the center of attention and was loved by many. It was often challenging for me to deny the obvious when the unspoken silence of Farhad's disappearance and the family's fear of his whereabouts would surface, but I would stay focused on my goal of signing the papers that would provide a brighter future for him in Canada. I was convinced that my responsibility only extended up until the giving of my signatures and his care and well-being outside of this task was not on my conscience.

June 21st, 2007 was a bright and sunny Thursday and would be etched in my memory as the day of my first wedding. It was the day of the Summer Solstice, the longest day of the year and ironically also one of the longest days of my life. We rented a private studio where baba and I did a pre-wedding photoshoot. What couple performing a visa marriage would spend the time and money to do a pre-wedding family photoshoot? Because it is illegal for a woman to be uncovered in public, it was an indoor studio and our pictures were in front of a green screen, which after much tacky digital editing would transform into a photoshoot of baba and I in front of beautiful landscapes. This kind of editing was not meant to trick the Canadian government, this was an actual Iranian tactic used by all brides to get the dream photos they wanted in front of mountains and rivers with their beautiful hair-dos exposed, but unfortunately could not due to the restrictions imposed.

Farhad had a long-term girlfriend during the entire time that I was in Iran and I got to know her well during my time there. She was a sweet girl who was mature, had a full-time job, did not have a substance abuse issue like Farhad, and all these details about her left me wondering why she was with him and even more absurdly, why she was so deeply in love with him. On the morning of June 21st, she called me. Our conversations up until that day were cordial, pleasant, and I suppose a bit superficial. I was getting ready in the bathroom when I answered her call. She was sobbing on the other end of the line. I was surprised by the tears and immediately had my guard up. My first reaction to her sobbing was that Farhad was dead. I tried to calm her down so that I could understand the words that were intermittently spaced between her heavy breathing and wheezing for air because of her running nose probably from all the crying. Then I stopped speaking did what maman taught me best to do, listen. I listened for her words and her emotions. And it hit me so hard that I almost felt ashamed that I never understood her position before this morning as I was getting ready to marry her boyfriend. I realized that although I had assured her thousands of times that this was not a real wedding and she had nothing to worry about and that there was nothing going on romantically between Farhad and I, although we had clearly had this conversation many times, I had failed to comprehend it from her point of view on what this marriage meant for her. This marriage meant that the love of her life was going to be uprooted from her life and would be moving across oceans and to a country thousands of miles away. How was I so self-absorbed in finding my wings in Iran that I never even realized how my decision was going to impact her life? I slowly laid down on the bathroom floor, its cold tiles providing a much-needed relief to my flustered and warm face and we spoke for nearly three hours. It was the first time I felt the weight of my actions and my ability to impact the lives of people around me. It was a lesson maman and baba subtly were teaching us our entire lives and now it was my time to put that into action. It was the day of my fake wedding, but in that moment, the only thing that mattered was listening to her concerns and reassuring her that everything would be okay.

After the fake studio photoshoot for my fake wedding, I met Farhad at the legal office where the Islamic marriage would take place. My grandfather gave me a gold coin for a present. How funny is that? I was getting expensive and sincere gifts for my fake wedding! The Islamic marriage license has somewhat of a prenuptial that is integrated. It prescribes what the bride would be entitled to in the event of a divorce. My parents had a symbolic gesture and their license stated that maman would get a dozen roses from baba in the event of a divorce. I can't remember what my prenup agreement stated. I just went through the motions and gestures and signed in the places that were pointed to me by the big old religious leaders in their turbans and long beards. And before I knew it, I was signing on the last dotted line which transferred my ownership from my father to now my husband. The tall, bearded, and turbaned men were now congratulating us.

We all returned to Farhad's grandma's upstairs apartment that I was staying in for the last 3 months, for the wedding reception and pictures. We had decorated the apartment and I had decided that if I was going to get married, that I deserved a party. There were mountains of delicious Iranian food, lots of alcohol, close family, and friends that we trusted with the truth of this marriage, and a lot of music and dancing. Between all the dancing and getting heavily drunk from the home made wine and questionable vodka, there was no time to think about what had just happened. I had legally entered into a marriage to a man that I hardly knew, with a loving girlfriend who cared deeply for him, who did not have a job or an income or any sense of responsibilities, and had a serious substance abuse problem. I was dancing and jumping, intoxicated out of my mind and in one of my blurry panoramic glances across the room of the guests sitting around the edges and watching me and few of my cousins dancing, I wondered what they thought of me. A drunk Canadian girl with 38DD breasts flying up and down since I refused to wear a bra with my wedding dress, and just then one of the spaghetti straps snapped.

Towards the end of the night, I finally sat on the dining table and I got myself a plate of food to eat in the hopes of absorbing some of the alcohol. Farhad was sitting next to me and as he always did was smoking a cigarette. Both of us drunk, sitting beside each other as husband and wife but not having a single word to say to each other. I quietly anticipated a "merci" from Farhad, as I was sure he would thank me at least once or acknowledge some type of appreciation for my gesture. Merci was one of the French words adopted in Farsi culture as a casual way to express gratitude. Farhad finished his cigarette and extinguished the bud on my dinner plate that I was still working on. I sarcastically said, "you're welcome", in my mind. That was who Farhad had become, ungrateful, disrespectful, and ignorant to what all these people in the room had done for him and orchestrated so that he could have a better life. This was now my dear husband.

My New Chapter

My debt to my family was paid, and I was ready to selfishly focus on new goals with my newfound confidence in Iran. I got accepted into Mohawk College for an advertising diploma program and jumped into the deep end ready to take in everything that it had to offer. Just like ten years ago when my family first arrived in Canada and we left behind our lives in Iran, a decade later I was once again leaving Iran and with it my marriage and my anger towards Farhad, his ungratefulness and the events of that wedding night. I had made the decision on my own, and unaffected by anyone's judgement that I would not be pursuing a University degree, but rather settling for a college diploma. I was taking control of my life and writing my destiny. Little did I know how much I would fall in love with advertising and the places and opportunities that it would present to me. I had new friends, teachers, textbooks to read, and a whole new life. And in this carefully curated new life, there was no place for mention of Farhad, my marital status or any other baggage that lingered with me. Farhad and I never exchanged any more words with each other after our wedding night where he disrespectfully put out his cigarette on my dinner plate. Baba and Nazee promised to take care of all the administrative paperwork and that I wouldn't have to give up anything else for this marriage. I returned from Iran a queen in my home, there were no more arguments with Nazee, I could do no wrong, there was always peace in the house. And to this day, the status quo has not changed. My relationship with Nazee and Farnaz included one more title as a daughter-in-law and sister-in-law respectively. I quit all my prior negative thoughts of being a university drop out, I quit my previous part-time jobs for a new one, and I started to rebuild and write a new chapter in my life.

I enjoyed homework for the first time in my life. Baba even noticed this and would say with surprise, "Banoojaan, I've never seen you do so much homework before". I came to realize that it wasn't homework that I didn't like, it was doing homework that I didn't see value in or studying about topics that didn't pique my interest. Advertising had transformed my educational experience. I wanted to read every page of my textbooks and attentively participated in every one of my lectures. They say time flies when you're having fun, and there couldn't be truer words to describe my three years at Mohawk college. I had never learned more through any institutionalized education system, I had never been more inspired at the thought of a career, and I had never been more opportunistic about a bright future for myself. Maman and baba always emphasized the importance of education, and Mohawk college and the education that I received there solidified this lifelong family lesson in that there is freedom and autonomy that comes with pursuing a post-secondary education and especially pursuing a subject of deep passion and interest and then embracing the knowledge with childlike enthusiasm.

I was twenty-two years old and was offered an entry-level position at an exceptional ad agency in Toronto. Banafsheh from Bandar Abbas was moving to the big city. The three years at Mohawk College had re-wired my neuroreceptors. They had transformed my insecurities into confidence and had erased and blurred those parts of my previous life that previously made me feel ashamed. Moving to the big city, I looked, felt, and acted like an entirely different person. In Toronto, I started to meet other young ad professionals in an industry notorious for hyper socialization. I worked tirelessly, going above and beyond with every new project and account given to me. I would never hesitate to work on evenings and weekends to meet aggressive deadlines. This work would be followed by praise and recognition from my bosses and the agency. Bonuses, pay raises, and promised promotions started to come my way. And if I wasn't working, or sleeping, I was out with my new advertising peers spending all our money at various happy hours across the city.

My colleagues and I would stay out late at bars and discuss our various accounts, their creative needs, complain about demanding clients and unreasonable deliverables. This industry was like a drug and I was addicted to it. I lived, breathed, and dreamed advertising. I started to notice a strange yet familiar shift at bars and other social gatherings. I always knew that I enjoyed storytelling, but my hidden life and identity as a university drop-out, an unusual familiar setup, and even more unusual marriage had dampened my desire to tell stories. But in Toronto with my new friends, that part of my life was carefully packed and stored away and never reared it's ugly head.

I had found my voice and it was that of a storyteller. My friends always wanted to know more about my day.

"Violet, tell Mark about what your client asked you yesterday" or "Violet, when is your next promotion going to be?"

I would always find groups gravitating towards me at parties. Conversations very often converged around me speaking and subsequently reciting one of my many stories, but never about my marriage or the events of Iran. It was an odd experience of déjà vu. In the beginning, I wasn't sure if it was the tipsiness of a few beers that gave me that feeling like I had been here in this same position so many times before.

It was as if I was having an out of body experience - observing myself from outside of myself. And then one day it finally came to me. It's that feeling when you're racking your brains to place a silly detail. You can feel it and see it, but just can't verbalize it. Sometimes when I meet clients that I worked with several months ago and I'm trying to trace all the connections in my brain to remember their name and it will be hours later on the subway ride back to my apartment that I remember it. My realization of the familiarity of my new social conversations, setup, and geometry had hit me just like that.

I was my maman's daughter.

As a young girl in Bandar Abbas running around the bazaar on my birthday with maman grabbing the supplies for my party, we would be stopped by people all the time. They all wanted to give their greeting to maman, ask her for advice, hear about her day and just listen to her speak. Maman was the center of all family parties. I could never step into the shoes of a master's in engineering, top of her class, community leader like maman, but I think she sprinkled some of that charismatic, storytelling DNA into me. After six years of maman's passing, I finally felt her presence with me.

Just like maman's dedication to her work, I was committed to mine. Just like maman's desire to be a respected leader, I would go above and beyond to take people under my wing and bring my peers up with me. Just like maman's commitment to her community, I was devoted to my friends and started dedicating time and resources to social causes worth educating myself and fighting for. Toronto was shaping me into a driven and focused advertising professional. Almost four years since my "I do" in Iran, I had forgotten about Farhad, my marriage to him and that entire chapter of my life. And then one evening when I was at Bahar's house, she inquired about Farhad's visa status and when I shrugged it off as none of my business, she said three sentences that would pull me right back down to earth from the cloud on which I was floating for the last year.

"Banoo, you will need to stand in front of the government of Canada and express financial and legal responsibility for this man. It is your signature on the marriage license. It's been almost four years, aren't you concerned?".

In less than thirty seconds, I was that nineteen-year-old-university-drop-out-Violet. My anxiety had returned and all evening I would let my paranoia get the better of me and run through every possible negative outcome. Having to financially support Farhad. Being charged by the Canadian government. Being jailed for marriage fraud. Returning to Iran and being forced to live there as his wife. I couldn't take it anymore. I was not willing to ruin everything that I had built for myself and my career over the last four years to be stripped away from me. The next day I went to baba and Nazee's house and we had a "family meeting". I wanted answers and I didn't dance around the topic. I asked, "Nazee arrived in Canada in less than a year after you married her, baba, so why was it taking so long for Farhad to get his visa?" Baba and Nazee weren't hiding the details from me to be sneaky, but they genuinely wanted to keep their promise to me of never having to think or deal with this marriage arrangement. I learnt that he couldn't pass the Canadian visa application medical examinations. Why was a twenty-nine-year-old young man not able to pass a medical examination? And for four years? How many medical examinations had he failed? Does he have a chronic health condition? And do I need to support his medical bills in Canada if he has a chronic medical condition? Like I said, I wanted answers. I got some and some remained unresolved. No one was willing to admit why he wasn't passing his medical exams because the reality of what happens to a human body from years of substance abuse was not something that was discussed within the four walls of a traditional Iranian home. Baba asked me just one question towards the end of our heated conversation. "Banoojaan, what do you want to do?". Unlike the time when I agreed to marry Farhad without any thought, this time around I was different. I was nervous to say something that would reverse my relationship with Nazee and all the goodwill that had resulted from marrying her son. But I was also a college graduate with a bright future ahead of me and filled with the confidence and eloquence of maman. And I said the five words and would end that evening's "family meeting".

"Baba, I want a divorce".

Divorce Papers

The very next morning I started to research what I needed to do to cancel the visa application. Although their intentions to protect me and not cause me any more inconvenience with this marriage was kind and appreciated, I couldn't leave any of this to baba and Nazee any longer. I found the mailing address for the Ministry of Immigration by navigating the complicated Government of Canada website. I typed up a brief letter stating my intentions to cancel my spousal immigration application, sealed, and mailed it out the very same day. At the time I was living in Toronto and renting a room in a two-bedroom apartment, and my roommate was a lovely girl named Diana. We lived your stereotypical big city, early twenties, life. Weekends very often involved last minute plans of friends and colleagues coming over for an impromptu house party. A few weeks had passed since I mailed in my visa cancellation request. It was just before one of the last-minute Friday gatherings that I decided to check the mail. The government of Canada had written back to me. I quickly grabbed the letter and ran into my room. This new life that I had in Toronto was intentionally crafted to be disjoint in every aspect from my previous life. These people who were now in my living room, drinking and setting up for a game of beer pong, had no idea about my alternate, yet parallel life and the marriage to my cousin in Iran While Diana was lovely, I could not imagine innocently admitting that a few years ago I had married my cousin, who is also my step-brother, to get him a visa in to Canada. My new friends would never understand that, and why would they, when my new identity could hardly approve of what I had done. I held the letter in my hand, trying to block out the cheering noises from outside of my room, and Diana's intermittent checks at my door, for when I would be joining our guests. I opened the letter and read the first two lines,

"Dear Ms. Banafsheh Karbalaei,

We have received your letter, and this is to notify you that your spousal application has been cancelled."

I cried big heavy tears of joy and relief. I no longer had to explain to the Canadian immigration officer about why the pre-wedding photoshoot with baba in front of mountains and rivers looked fake and staged. I wouldn't have to explain the sexist "Sugar Rubbing" ceremony either. I closed my eyes, said an atheist's prayer, and decided to get drunk that night. Diana and my friends had no idea why I was even more euphoric than my usual self. As always, they would ask me questions about my day and my clients and with a big glass of wine in my hand and an even bigger smile on my face, I recited back to them my stories in classic maman style.

I knew the uphill battle was not complete yet. The next goal was to officially get the Islamic divorce for which I needed baba and his connections in Iran who could maneuver the corrupt and bureaucratic court system to get my letter of freedom. I thought of how baba had to slip the bribe envelope to the immigration officer for our Canadian visas and I was irritated at the thought of having to spend money to get this huge inconvenience sorted out. But I was determined and ready to cut all legal, financial, and if needed even familial ties with Farhad to get my divorce. I disliked my dependence on baba for resolving this piece of the puzzle, but acknowledged my limitations of being in Canada. However, I didn't shy away from repeatedly pestering baba and Nazee for updates on the divorce papers that seemed to encounter one hurdle after another. Months turned into almost a full year and I still didn't have the divorce papers. Every so often when I would get fired up for answers, I would call baba with my litany of questions and that's when I learnt that Farhad's dad got divorced from his second wife as well, which didn't surprise me too much since she seemed too kind and virtuous of a woman to be with someone like him. And the latest news was that Farhad and his dad were officially missing. Nobody in Tehran knew of their whereabouts. Since our wedding night and the cigarette incident, and subsequently throughout the prolonged visa and divorce process, my feelings towards Farhad transitioned into nothing more than that of a stranger that I was trying to get rid of from my life. So, the father-son missing person's report didn't make me react with worry or concern, but more with annoyance that the courts couldn't find him and now this was going to delay the divorce process even further. To my surprise I found out that there was a law for if a person is trying to get a divorce from their partner but is unable to locate their partner to get their signature. Makes me wonder, how often people find themselves in this situation, warranting a formal and legal law written for it. The law states that the person seeking the divorce must print an ad in the local newspaper three times requesting for the whereabouts of the missing spouse. And if there is no response to all three of these ads, the party seeking the divorce will be granted one by the courts.

Around this time, a new idea came to my family, and they advised me that it would be better to annul the marriage than getting a divorce so that the record could be entirely erased. Farhad and I never shared a home together, never shared financial responsibilities together, and never consummated the marriage, which were the requirements to legally and religiously, since they are the same in Iran, annul a marriage. This seemed like a great option that even made me happy that I hadn't gotten the divorce earlier because if I did, then this option would not be available. We immediately got Nazee and maman's younger brother involved. He was a lawyer in Tehran and his firm would assist me with the annulment. One evening, soon after we had decided to proceed down the annulment path, baba informed me that a lawyer from my uncle's firm wanted to speak to me. Knowing Iran's cultural treatment of women, the rights of women, and especially those trying to annul their marriages to "good" Muslim men, I foreshadowed the conversation would be a frustrating one. To protect my sanity, I refused to speak to the lawyer but agreed to let her send me an email with her questions. Very promptly the next morning I had an email in my inbox. It was a long email that was written in eloquent Farsi. Farsi is my mother tongue; it's what baba and I converse in and I am fluent in the language. But somehow the complex words and the legal jargon of this email made me feel like I had been speaking a fraudulent version of the language my entire life. It took me almost three times of slowly and carefully reading the email to fully understand what was being asked of me. And I also realized that the reason I wasn't understanding it was because the request made no logical sense at all.

This Iranian lawyer, in her grand wisdom, wanted me to get a pregnancy test done. Furthermore, they wanted an M.D to authorize that I was in fact not pregnant at this very moment. And they needed this official letter of authorization from a medical doctor to annul my marriage? How did any of this make sense, considering my marriage was almost five years ago? And more importantly which Canadian doctor in their sane and educated mind would produce such a ridiculous document for me? Desperate for the annulment, I was willing to go to any lengths to acquire this freedom. I decided to go into a walk-in clinic, avoiding the shame of requesting this from my family doctor in Toronto who I was sure thought of me as a responsible and wise young ad professional and I didn't think it wise to approach him with this absurd request. The physician at the clinic was beyond perplexed by my request. I begged and pleaded and try to explain to this very well-mannered and Canadian educated Caucasian doctor why I needed an authorized letter that I was not pregnant at the current moment to annul a visa marriage from nearly five years ago.

Channeling my inner maman and her story telling charm, I convinced this doctor to give me a pregnancy test, verify the results, and produce this document. I am sure he tells his friends about this Iranian walk-in patient's ridiculous request at his lovely dinner parties and backyard barbeques. Embarrassed and relieved, I rushed out of the clinic, quickly took a picture of the letter and sent it off to my lawyer in Iran hoping the legal system's minimal understanding of how pregnancies occur and my letter of confirmation that I was not pregnant would do the trick. Because it would truly be a magic trick if my marriage to Farhad would yield a pregnancy with him almost five years later, while we lived in two separate continents. Two days later, the second email request would appear in what read like even more complicated Farsi with an even more absurd request. Since I am an Iranian-Muslim woman, and in Islamic law a woman can only have sexual relations inside of a marriage. And since I've only been married once and claiming that we never consummated the marriage, the logical conclusion drawn by the Iranian courts is that I am a virgin. While I was beside myself with the request, I did agree that this logic in theory at least made more sense than their previous one. And in very detailed and sophisticated Farsi my lawyer asked me to produce an authentic certificate of virginity. I was enraged! My feminist-educated-social justice warrior-Canadian mind exploded in laughter and anger simultaneously. It was a Wednesday morning; I was sitting at my cubicle surrounded by my young and progressive ad colleagues who were entirely unaware of the annulment that I was pursuing from my cousin and stepbrother. But I couldn't hide my emotions as I burst out into a laughing rage as I read the most ridiculous email that I had received in my life!

There was no way that I was going into a medical clinic, spreading apart my legs so that the physician could provide me with a certificate of virginity. Firstly, I was pretty sure that it's illegal to request or dispense such a certificate. Secondly, I highly doubt a Canadian doctor would be so medically naïve to think the "hymen" test was in fact hundred percent accurate. And lastly, I was not a virgin. The rage I was experiencing tangentially transitioned from one topic to another and before I knew it, I was preparing my speech for the Supreme Leader of Iran condemning his anti-woman regime and systemic oppression of women. My Wednesday had barely started, and I was ready to set this world on fire. So, after a couple weeks of what seemed like a promising option of pursuing an annulment, I was back to square one and requesting for a divorce.

In a few days the first ad was printed in the newspapers requesting for Farhad to identify himself so that Banafsheh could get her divorce. There was no response. After the obligatory wait for a couple of weeks, the second ad was printed. There was no response. And finally, a few weeks after the first ad was printed, the third and last ad was sent to the local newspaper. Not surprising to anyone, there was no response again.

Since my last trip to Iran, which is when I got married, I had not returned to visit Iran. My family and friends that I had grown so fond of during the wedding period yearned to see me as did I to see them. Per Iranian law a woman's ownership transitions from her father to her husband upon her marriage. And according to this ownership, Farhad could detain me, if he pleased, on Iranian soil by requesting the airport border officers to confiscate my passport and so denying me exit from the country. It had been almost five years of this involuntary possession and control that he could exercise over me. While baba and Nazee would often go back, I was always afraid to accompany them from the fear to being unable to return to Canada. All the close friendships and relations that I had nurtured during my last visit to Iran were on hold and started to fade once again like they had the first time around when my family immigrated to Canada. When I left Iran after my marriage in 2007, I had vowed my friends and family to not let that happen again, but without possession of the signed divorce papers, I was too afraid to risk my freedom by entering Iran. It was the country that I was born in, that my parents and their parents were born in, but generations of that bond were diluted down by patriarchal norms and laws. Expecting to be granted the divorce according to the law, because of Farhad's lack to response to my newspaper ads, I waited for a few more weeks and finally just before my twenty-fifth birthday, baba called me and gave me the news.

"Banoojaan, you're a free woman. I have the signed divorce papers".

Meeting the Devil

The Farhad chapter of my life was over.

I was free.

I was legally single.

I never asked baba of any details on how and what happened to get the divorce. Did they find Farhad and get his signature? Did the court grant the divorce based on the newspaper ads? I didn't ask, and I couldn't have cared less at the time as I felt five years of handcuffs release from my wrists and a permanent sense of anxiety and claustrophobia lifted out of my chest. I felt lighter. My first act as a single woman was to take a solo trip to somewhere I hadn't been before and I decided to visit maman's brother, Amoo Farjad and my cousins in Vancouver. I told my cousin about wanting a new start in my career, in a different country and how I was especially drawn to London, England. I had visited the city many times before and had a few connections that I could count on. We spoke all night about moving to London and primarily her trying to convince me to make the move and get the new start that I was looking for. I had three main fears – "What if I can't find a job? What if I can't find a nice place to live? What if I don't make any friends there?" By now, my roommate, Diana, and I were close friends and over the year, I had heard of and met a lot of her family members including one of Diana's aunt, Susan, who lived in Mexico City and coincidentally had very close contacts in the advertising industry in London.

When I told Diana about my itch to move to London and my fear about getting a job, she immediately connected me and Susan and in just one short conversation Susan immediately assured me that her network was extensive in London and that I had nothing to worry about regarding a job. My first fear had resolved.

I had a friend, Luke, who had moved to London a few years ago and so I called him to see what the rental marker situation was like in London, what the payments were like, how early do places come up for rent, best neighbourhoods to live and work in and he very quickly sensed my anxiety building around a place to live in a foreign country and city. He stopped me partway through my rant of questions and concerns and said, "Violet, you're going to be staying with me". Turns out Luke was signing the papers for a new two bedroom flat and he generously asked me to stay with him until I got settled in the city. My second fear had resolved.

I was almost over the fence with making the decision to move to London and I decided to call my friend Carla in Montreal. Carla and I met many years ago through friends of friends, became very close and visited London for the first time together, several years ago and have remained close confidants ever since. I was calling to tell Carla about my potential change in address, and before I could even start to tell my story and just as we were saying our hellos and I was asking her how she was doing, she excitedly gives me her big news, "Violet, I'm moving to London". Huh? That was my news! Carla had been deliberating a move for months and was looking for a fresh start as well. She was ahead of me by a couple of months because she had applied for her visa and had just received it in the mail earlier that morning. My final fear had resolved. I would have a job, a place to live, and close friends with me. I don't know why I was nervous to tell baba about my decision, because he had never given me a reason to believe that he would constrain me from pursuing my dreams and aspirations, but maybe I drew a parallel between wanting to quit my well-paying and stable career in Toronto to dropping out of university all those years ago. "Banoojaan, anything that you put your heart to you will succeed at, and if moving to London is your dream, I support you fully". In typical fashion of quote Rumi, he shared one of his favourite verses, "You were born with wings, why prefer to crawl through life?" I felt silly worrying about all of those other fears of a job, and a place to live, and friends for support, because as those words came out of baba I immediately knew that they were all I needed to make this leap. The decision was made, and I was moving to London.

My best friend, Linda, threw me a going away party with London themed decorations and foods and some of my closest friends. The day of the party, one of our friends wrote a poem for me.

Violet *– 50% red, 50% blue.*
You can add a bit of one or the other to change the hue for you.
Violet *– A plant family, in fact one of my favourites;*
With flowers of all shades in pink, purple, and blue.
Violet *– The piercing sparkle of the precious stone amethyst;*

Violet – *what comes to mind as I think of the sweet smell of lavender mist.*

Violet – *the fastest traveling wavelength in the visible light spectrum, or what we call a rainbow;*

It's so special that the spectrum after is named in its honour or ultraviolet, as we know.

Violet – *Colour psychologists associate it with representing the future, one's dreams, and imagination,*

Violet – *it's also the colour for royalty, spirituality, and long-term vision.*

Violet – *the perfect combination of two syllables. The first one strong & fierce – "Vi" – vivacious, vigor, victor, valiant, viable;*

The second one so natural – "Let" – like a dropLet of water that gives life, an outLet of blood to survive.

Violet – *my dearest, names are so important to speak of one's identity and boast of one's character;*

But I wonder how your parents as they looked at their infant knew she would embody the litany of significances of the name they were giving her.

Violet – *this was always your destiny from the day you were born and the day that you were named;*

Violet – *you were meant to fly, dream, and achieve,*

And doing anything but that, would be oh! What a shame.

My eyes sparkled from the tears that were forming because I was going to leave behind all these incredible friends of mine, and I also silently chuckled because my friend had no idea that my name was Banafsheh. Violet had been my identity in this country for over a decade and I was in a constant state of duality between Banafsheh at home and Violet, my alter ego. Some part of me thought of Violet as a scam and not authentic because those that called me it didn't know my true story, but for the first time looking around the kitchen at Linda's home where we were gathered and just heard the recitation of a poem written for me, I felt proud of Violet.

Maman and baba had taught me the importance to taking risks and the freedom that you earn when you become the author of your life. "It's in these leaps, Banoojaan", baba would say, "that we find the opportunities that we yearn for". Baba and maman knew this, and their leap to Canada was in search of that opportunity. The freedom for their children to pursue any career and life that they wished for. The freedom to enjoy their livelihoods without fear of prostate cancer or a glioblastoma bankrupting them and their families.

I quickly found a job in London, and a two-bedroom apartment with Carla. A random assortment of work friends, Luke, and Carla had become my new family. Weekdays were cramped with learning about the London ad industry and charming my peers and bosses with my Canadian "eh" after every sentence and sharing anecdotes of life as an ad professional in Toronto. Turns out even the English enjoyed my stories and were always intrigued with what experience I would share next. My cubicle at work quickly became the pitstop for many on their way to the bathroom or the kitchen. The one year that I lived in London is to-date one of the best years of my life. It was an immediate release and freedom from the last decade of my life and from my always-present identity crisis. I had hardly finished a year in London and found that the job I was doing wasn't where I wanted it to be in my career. So, when a previous boss reached out and offered me a promotion back in Toronto, I leaped, again. I had soaked myself with love, friendship, experiences, and memories in London and was ready to return to my life and career in Toronto. I was a bit disappointed that my stay wasn't longer, or more permanent, but by that time in my life, I also knew that nothing was permanent.

For someone not raised in a religious or spiritual home, maman and baba's actions and discussions always had strong lessons rooted in existential themes of life and purpose.

The disappointment quickly turned into relief and happiness. Only a few months after I returned to Canada, baba and Nazee decided to move back to Iran for their retirement. I knew that once they left, I would only see them a couple of times a year if I could squeeze in 1-2 visits to Iran annually. For the next several months, before they left, I visited them every weekend, and soaked in all the time I could get with baba. I didn't miss any opportunity to reminisce old memories with him, and squeezed in every second with the man who introduced me to the science of gravity when I was four and every other lesson that I have learned since then. I took comfort in knowing that our gravitational attraction as being objects with mass, in theory, could extend across continents. And more importantly, technology afforded us to stay as connected as we chose. And before I knew it, on a cool fall day in September, I ordered a taxi for baba, Nazee and I to take us, and their luggage, to the airport. Baba insisted there was no need for me to come along, but he and I both knew this was more for me than for him. Canada is where I got my first job and earned my first paycheck, where I learned a completely new language, fell in love with its vocabulary, where I discovered my love for advertising, and established a successful career, where my character was shaped and I had discovered how similar I was to maman, where I made friendships that were going to last a lifetime, and where my maman had taken her last breath. Baba standing there, having sold his home and all his belongings, for the second time in his life, ready to walk through the check-in gates, reminded me of everything I had achieved in Canada. I stood looking into the eyes of the man who made all of that happen for me. Both of our eyes were welled up and we stood in silence for a few moments. I asked him to give me all the advice that he could give me, as quickly as possible, before he walked through the gates. In typical baba fashion, with the gentlest of smiles, on a face that was now etched with graceful wrinkles, he said, "Banoojaan, I am so proud of you and the person that you have become. You are kind, intelligent and caring. You are just like your maman and she would also be so proud of you". We hugged, he kissed me, and walked towards Nazee, who was waiting closer to the gate. I watched them as they crossed over to the other side. It was one of the saddest and happiest days of my life. Baba was returning to his homeland. While he was full of gratitude for Canada, never regretting his decision to move his family, his gentle heart had always been in Iran. It's smells and colours he missed deeply, the dry heat he only dreamed of now, the people, the music, the hookah by the beach, and the garlic infused kebabs awaited him on the other side of that gate. I couldn't be happier for baba to get this opportunity to retire in the land that he loved, but I never understood why they made the decision to leave so quickly and abruptly. I presumed it was because of old age, and how it reminded people of their finite time on earth, and so everyday spent not doing what you were meant to, seemed like a steep price to pay.

Bahar was living in Hamilton with her husband and their two sons and Farnaz was living with her family in Burlington. Although, I lived in Toronto and didn't have my driver's license, I would come back to Hamilton every weekend to spend time with both of them. Our parents had left, and I wanted to keep the remaining pieces of our Canadian family together, as best I could.

I video chatted with baba almost daily to hear about their lives and he would show me the farmhouse they were living in with fig trees and the mountains on one side and the beach on the other. It reminded me of Amoo Farjad's farmhouse in Sari that we would visit with Farhad. Nine months after their departure, in May, I was video chatting with baba one evening and he was showing me the chicken they were raising on their property and although I have no affinity for chicken or livestock I realized how much I missed baba. I hung up the phone and booked a ticket to Iran immediately. It had been almost a decade since I was last in Iran for my wedding. A lot had happened since that visit, but my confirmed divorce to Farhad put me at ease that I had nothing to fear about and I was ready to go back. I booked my ticket in a hurry, got my vacation approved with my boss, and was ready for my big trip. It was the weekend before my flight, and per our custom I was going over to Bahar's home to spend time with my nephews and say my goodbyes and I called Farnaz to see if she was available meet at Bahar's place. She didn't answer her phone and so I left her a text message as well. Completely orthodox to Farnaz's kind and considerate manners, she never called me back or texted me back. I proceeded to call her and text her multiple times and when there was still no response, my final text was a cry for attention, as I asked her if she was alive? She immediately called me back, and the sound of her "Hello" instantly heightened my awareness and I knew that something was wrong. In a full body breakdown, she said, "Farhad just died". Silence. One second, two seconds, three seconds, four seconds. Silence. I didn't know what and how to feel and there were no words that came to my lips. Silence. My cousin had died. My stepbrother, and Nazee's son was gone. My ex-husband had died. Silence. I know in the last decade there was more than once that I swore at him or wished him ill. I had negative memories of his last interactions with me, and how he took years to grant me my divorce. I know I did. But now, he was gone. Silence. I must have said something back to Farnaz because I had hung up the phone and I was hazily making my way into Bahar's living room to give her the news. And we both sat together and cried. Farhad was the antagonist of my life's story for so many years. My tears were for Farnaz's, Bahar's, and Nazee's loss.

Two days later, I had boarded my flight to Iran and my excitement to spend time with baba had quickly transitioned into the anxiety of attending Farhad's funeral, comforting Nazee and being in a house that was mourning. Baba and Nazee's home were filled with pictures of Farhad, but there was no mourning. I was confused. Nazee shared a few stories but that was it, and every day they stayed focused on showing me around their new home and community and on making my visit to Iran a special one. She told me about how weak and frail her son's body had become through years of drug abuse and other consequential illnesses. I found out that for the last few years, Farhad was so sick that he would just sleep for days on end, and that he was sitting and eating an ice cream when his dad found him dead on the couch.

A few days later was baba's sixty-ninth birthday, the real reason for my rushed visit to Iran. Since it seemed like there was no mourning and that everyone was okay, I decided to have a celebration. I invited all my cousins, family, friends, and even Farhad's dad to the celebration. We went out to a fancy restaurant and I ordered kebabs, fresh bread, stews, saffron rice and after the meal was done they brought out hookahs for all of us to enjoy and I insisted on picking up the tab. This was my party for my baba's birthday, and I wanted to make sure that it was perfect. The next day after we all woke up at my grandparents' home slightly hungover, and I was sitting with a couple of my cousins and maman's cousin for breakfast and I casually mentioned how it was odd that nobody was mourning Fahad's death. My uncle went on to tell me how it was almost a relief that everyone felt at the news of his death. He spoke about Farhad not being a good person with a happy life. He didn't have a stable family, didn't have an education, didn't have a job, and his final few years was just a sick and bed ridden person that didn't accept anyone's help. He told me how Farhad and his dad even came and stayed with baba and Nazee for a few weeks so that they could take care of him. But he didn't get any better. And finally, his life of substance abuse and addiction caught up to him and ultimately took his life.

Like many cultures, there is a huge stigma against substance abuse in Iran, and my protected Canadian identity, sat there wondering how much of Farhad's story that my uncle recited could have been avoided by family support, community programs, and a good health care system. But it was certain by the end of that talk, Farhad's passing was not a shock but an expected and welcome relief for the family. For the first time since I heard of Farhad's death, I cried for my dear cousin.

Later that evening, while we were eating dinner, I started to hear bits and pieces of a conversation between my uncle and his cousin. The bits I heard were about Farhad's dad getting so tired of taking care of his dying son. They mentioned how Farhad was the only person left in the world that could bare to live with his dad. Both of his wives had left him, and he was a lonely and miserable person. Then suddenly, I heard my name "Banafsheh" in the conversation. Why were they talking about me? My attention entirely focused in on their conversation, "It's so awful what they put Mehdi and Nazee through". I didn't know how to react. What did that man do to my baba? I could no longer be a fly on the wall in that conversation and immediately leaped in and asked, "Amoo Farshad, what are you talking about". There are certain defining moments in a person's life. And when you experience one of these moments, it traces a line in your life story. There was life before that experience, and there was life after that experience. Moving to Canada was one of those traced lines. Agreeing to marry Farhad was another line. And this conversation with my uncle and his cousin was another traced line.

I was raised in a house full of love. Maman and baba showered us with so much kindness and love, that we never even learnt the word for 'hate' in Farsi. The emotion and experience of hate was something the cells in my brain never knew and never understood. And this conversation at the age of twenty-seven would teach me the emotion of hate for another human being.

My uncle told me about the miserable man that was Farhad's dad. He never cared for any person in his life and only worshipped one thing, and that was money. He left Nazee to protect his inheritance because nothing was more important than money. His second wife left him because he could never love her to the full extent like he loved wealth. No one could bear being around this man, except Farhad. And he corrupted Farhad's mind with all the wrong things and created a home devoid of any trace of love. "Banafsheh, do you know why your divorce took so many years? Your baba begged him over and over again for your freedom from his son." Farhad's dad tortured baba by holding my divorce ransom. And finally, baba had to surrender all his savings to pay off this man and buy my freedom and my divorce. Baba paid thousands of dollars and emptied his Canadian savings in return for the signed divorce papers. And that's why shortly after I received my divorce, baba and Nazee had to sell their town home in Canada and move back to Iran. Their retirement in Canada with their kids and grandkids was robbed from them by this monster. I always knew baba would give up his life for me. But I had no idea that my sixty-nine-year-old baba, who has never hurt a fly in his life, would be tortured and blackmailed for my sake.

I had finally met the devil and understood what it meant to hate someone. I hated them both. I cried and wept for baba and the torture that they put him through. I remember seeing pictures of Farhad's dad when he was younger, and I remember thinking that he was a good-looking man. But as he grew older, his face morphed into a version of the face of Lucifer that would you see in films. His eyes reflected evil, and his pores oozed envy and jealousy. He was the devil incarnate. How lonely and pitiful must someone be to treat others the way he had treated the people in his life. He had poisoned Farhad's life and my dear cousin had paid the ultimate price for that. I hated him with every cell in my body.

Could this outcome have been avoided if Farhad had received his visa to Canada?

Iran

Iran is home to one of the oldest civilizations. Even today, many Iranians will call themselves 'Persians' in pride of their rich history as one of the major powers of the ancient world. The word, paradise, has its origins in Persian, meaning "enclosed garden", and it's not surprising that Iranians consider their land and their civilization to be the promised paradise. When you strip away political agendas, religious corruption, and centuries of patriarchy, there lies a fabled land between the Caspian Sea, the

Persian Gulf, and the Gulf of Oman. On this rugged and mountainous terrain, are bustling cities like Tehran, Bandar Abbas, and Rasht filled with bazaars of people bargaining to get fair prices for beautiful Persian rugs, dried figs, spices, and everything else in between. While the streets are filled with women covered from head to toe, and public spaces separated for women and men, inside their homes are colourful masquerade parties overflowing with cheap booze and lots of dancing. This is the land where baba and maman met, fell in love, and where I was born. Their marriage was the epitome of relationships, inspired by a strong culture of respect, and rhythmic verses of famous Persian poets. It is by the port of Bandar-Abbas that I learned about the innate gravitational force between all objects which has stayed in my mind to this day as the reason that I feel so intensely drawn to the needs, joys, happiness, and sadness of people around me. This rich soil of Iran has cultivated crops that have formed my strong pallet for spices and a wide range of flavour foods. And on this fertile soil covered with orchards of fig trees, my cousin Farhad and I played for hours. When I was five, and he was ten, climbing up on one of these fig trees, in this beautiful country, I developed my first innocent crush on a boy. But Farhad would die a victim to this same land. How can a ground so rich in heritage, culture, and values, also be a sinkhole of lost talent and opportunity? A country with no gainful employment for so many of their youth, has led to millions wandering down a path of substance abuse and other poor and harmful choices.

What if maman survived her glioblastoma, and baba never married Nazee and brought her and Farnaz over to Canada? Would Farnaz have strolled down this same path? What if baba didn't seize the opportunity to immigrate to Canada all those years ago, would my rebellious state of repeatedly landing at the principal's office lead to dropping out of school and pursuing alternate lifestyles?

A famous Roman African playwriter, Publius Terentius Afer, wrote, "*Homo sum, humani nihil a me alienum puto*", or "I am human, and I think nothing human is alien to me." By virtue of being human, whatever good and bad that is experienced by another human cannot be alien to me and can very well be experienced by me. Farhad's decisions with his body and mind cannot be alien to me. Farhad's dad's choices of repeatedly pursuing wealth over relationships and forcing baba into buying my freedom cannot be alien to me. Maman's passion for helping her neighbour and community cannot be alien to me. And baba's desire to provide an opportunity for Nazee, Farnaz, and Farhad by bringing them to Canada cannot be alien to me.

There is no telling what intersections we'll encounter in our lives, and which road each of us will take. Baba and Nazee live on an amazing piece of land twenty minutes outside of Tehran. They are surrounded by greenery and have forty chickens freely running around on their property. Their days are filled with feeding and caring for their livestock and taking long walks amongst the rice fields. Baba started a business to rebuild his retirement funds and now has a few people working for him. Baba and Nazee can decide, on any given day, if they want to go to the beach or the forest. They are enjoying their life, while keeping some healthy distance from everyone else. Rebuilding one's life at sixty-nine can be a challenging task, but baba never backed down from a challenge. Even when his judo coach told him to stay away from the women in the class, it would not stop baba from pursuing the most beautiful woman in that class.

Bahar got her PhD and as my nephews grow old and mouthy, I'm constantly told that they take after their aunt Banooleh. Kasra is engaged to a beautiful and lovely woman and they are getting married next year. Baba and Nazee will be coming to Canada for the wedding. My uncle and his family from Vancouver will be coming for the wedding. And all my Iranian community in Canada that has supported my family for all these years will be celebrating with us. I'll be inviting my closest friends from high school, Linda, and Candace, to the party as well. We are all going to eat garlic-rubbed kebabs, drink cheap booze, and dance the night away.

The human spirit is often tried and tested with poisonous actions of people, aching losses, and devastating heart breaks. Maman is gone, and baba is thousands of miles away. But I will never forget the words of the poet, Rumi, "Do not feel lonely, the entire universe is inside you". I remember this verse and can't help but smile.

Acknowledgements

I would like to thank Violet for graciously offering to share her story with me, and to allow me the creative freedom to craft and recite it in my choice of colour and style. I cannot wait to travel with you to Iran one day and experience the beautiful landscapes that I have written about in this book.

A big THANK YOU to all the sisters in my life, who are always supporting my goals, inspiring me to see the wonder that surrounds me, and driving me to seek the truth.

About the Author

Celine is an Indian Canadian, who immigrated with her parents, Rena and George, and older sister, Rose, to Canada in 2001. Born in Cochin and raised in Mumbai until her move to Canada at the age of twelve, she is a lover of travel and exploring diverse cultures. A mechanical engineer by education, Celine is passionate about storytelling and especially the ones of extraordinary women like Violet. While she has previously dabbled in poetry and short essays, this is Celine's first book. Hope you will enjoy the read, as much as she enjoyed it's creation.

Manufactured by Amazon.ca
Bolton, ON